BEING HINDU

BEING HINDU

Understanding a Peaceful Path in a Violent World

Hindol Sengupta

ROWMAN & LITTLEFIELD
Lanham • Boulder • New York • London

Published by Rowman & Littlefield
An imprint of The Rowman & Littlefield Publishing Group, Inc.
4501 Forbes Boulevard, Suite 200, Lanham, Maryland 20706
www.rowman.com

86-90 Paul Street, London EC2A 4NE

British Library Cataloguing in Publication Information Available

Library of Congress Cataloging-in-Publication Data

Names: Sengupta, Hindol, author.
Title: Being Hindu : understanding a peaceful path in a violent world / Hindol
  Sengupta.
Description: Lanham : ROWMAN & LITTLEFIELD, 2017. | Originally published:
  Haryana, India : Penguin Books, 2015. | Includes bibliographical references and
  index.
Identifiers: LCCN 2017023126 (print) | LCCN 2017045703 (ebook) | ISBN
  9781442267466 (electronic) | ISBN 9781538193907 (paperback) | ISBN
  9781442267459 (hardback : alk. paper)
Subjects: LCSH: Hinduism.
Classification: LCC BL1202 (ebook) | LCC BL1202 .S33 2017 (print) | DDC 294.5—
  dc23
LC record available at https://lccn.loc.gov/2017023126

♾️™ The paper used in this publication meets the minimum requirements of
American National Standard for Information Sciences—Permanence of Paper
for Printed Library Materials, ANSI/NISO Z39.48-1992.

To my parents and Ishira

By all outward appearances our life is a spark of light between one eternal darkness and another.

—Alan W. Watts, *The Wisdom of Insecurity*

CONTENTS

PREFACE

Being Hindu is a book many told me not to write. Writing about religion is tricky in a world where offence is given, and taken, all too easily.

Writing about Hinduism is especially daunting because there is really nothing that can be said about it in broad, blanket, generic terms. What was once said about 'the East' by colonial writers is particularly true about Hinduism—everything, at once, seems true and untrue, every example has a counterexample, every history a different narrative.

But I was resolute that a new story of Hinduism needed to be told at a time when the faith of more than a billion people was being reimagined in many ways, both at home in India and around the world, with a new generation of practitioners using new approaches, ideologies, and technologies to access this ancient faith.

In India, there was a certain material journey to this. As the country of around eighty percent Hindus became wealthier, there was greater interest in the question of identity, and in India, identity has always been near inseparable from religion.

This quest for identity is not merely personal but extends to the surrounding community and, in turn, to the idea of India as a nation. While Being Hindu is the journey of individual seeking and understanding, it does hint at the overlap of this quest into wider societal queries and indeed politics, which took me a decade to understand and resulted in my latest book Soul and Sword: The Endless Battle over Political Hinduism, a history of political Hinduism that elaborates the scope for the transition I started ten years ago from the personal to the political.

In *Being Hindu*, however, the questions and answers are philosophical and contemplative rather than sociological or political, at least mostly so. Hinduism's diversity has meant countless ways in which seekers, old and new, access its wisdom and processes to build narratives about their lives, their country, and the broader world around them. What sages of yore accomplished through devout and dedicated pilgrimages, mapping the cartography of the land with their footsteps and gathering knowledge, many new seekers and gurus seek to achieve through cable television, then the mobile phone.

This churn was seen by some as opportunity and by others as threat. Moribund analysis, old diatribes, and even moulding histories about Hinduism were dissected, re-examined, and challenged. If there were reigning 'thought-leaders' in this ancient faith, they were questioned more than ever before.

Also asked was—what did it *mean* to be a Hindu? What was the relevance of all its monastic wisdom and revelations of forest-dwelling sages in the age of artificial intelligence? What role could Hinduism, which itself seemed so multitudinous, play in an increasingly fractured world?

So, I wrote a book on identity, mine, and how the Hindu faith had impacted my life, how this changed over the years, and lessons I had drawn from it. Through the experiences of one person—from a family as devotional as mine—I sought to tell a broader story of contemporary Hinduism and its place in the world. In my mind at least, this was a sort of a Gandhian endeavour to explore the understanding in oneself that one wished to see (about Hinduism) in the world.

It is now nearly a decade since I wrote *Being Hindu*, and its impact has astonished and delighted me. Not a week goes by when I do not receive mail or a text, often direct messages on social media, from readers who have enjoyed the book, who felt moved by it, and in whose lives *Being Hindu* has made a difference.

Many of the people who write to me about *Being Hindu*, especially from India, are in their twenties or thirties, and perhaps what works for them is the voice, the tonality, the inquisitiveness, and need for exploration that I have always felt. This might be unsurprising since I was in my early thirties when I wrote the book; it speaks to the curiosity and sense of 'figuring it all out' often common to that age.

One question that bothered me and which I addressed, in a somewhat cathartic manner, through *Being Hindu* is the question of free will about religion. Was it necessary for an individual, me in particular, to embrace the faith of my forefathers? To me, the answer has always seemed *no*— though it is an answer that my parents, like countless other Hindu, and dare I say other parents from other religions, were uncomfortable with. The book was, therefore, also a pathway and a process, often dialectical in nature, of trying to answer that question.

Hinduism, as I write in the book, is a bit like open-source software that consistently absorbs, assimilates, and presents new variants and versions, updates even, responding to societal needs and the urgencies of its followers. *Being Hindu* replicates that sense of openness and freedom in its deep dive into Hinduism. Perhaps this, in a world riddled with sectarian strife, led to it winning the Wilbur Award, the first book on Hinduism to win in seven decades.

Writing *Being Hindu* nudged me toward a path of writing other books on Hinduism, as I have gone deeper, trying to comprehend its vast universe. A reader once asked if writing *Being Hindu* made me a "better Hindu." I do not know about that, but as the book celebrates a decade in publication, I hope that it has at least made me a deeper seeker, a wider wanderer, and, hopefully, a better writer.

—Hindol Sengupta
December 2023

INTRODUCTION

Believer

I had finished this book and was starting the editing process when CNN began airing promos of the first episode of its *Believer* series with Muslim religious studies scholar Reza Aslan, who I had heard, in the past, making an eloquent case for the irreparable harm done by sensationalist depictions of Islam and some of its practices or passages in the Quran.

I tuned in eagerly hoping for a measured depiction of religious practices—something like National Geographic's *The Story of God*. Aslan, I thought, would naturally understand the need for thoughtfulness as a prominent campaigner against extremist depictions of religions using fringe practices.

But even the trailers deeply disappointed me. Aslan had shot in Benaras, one of the most holy places for the Hindus with its many sacred temples and bathing *ghats* (platforms), where thousands come to bathe in the holy river Ganga. The most ancient name of Benaras, and the one most commonly used by Hindus, is Kashi, literally meaning the City of Light. It is famous for its evening prayers with hundreds of oil lamps on the banks of the river and the festivity and color in each temple.

As the Harvard religious studies scholar Diana Eck noted in her book *Banaras: City of Light*, it is "a magnificent city"[1] (literally the first line of chapter 1 in her book) that for more than 2,500 years has attracted pilgrims and seekers from all around the world.

Riverside cremation happens on only two of Kashi's eighty-seven ghats. The burning of the dead bodies on wooden pyres, the immersion of the ashes in the holy river, and the temples in the background—all of this has given Hindus a sense of a relentless cycle of life.

But I was dismayed—not only did Aslan describe Benaras as the City of the Dead (he had clearly not even bothered to read Eck's renowned book, let alone any of the numerous famous books by Indian scholars about the city), he seemed not to have done even the most basic research—as basic as a Google search of the words *Benaras* and *ghats*. It took less than a minute on my laptop to search these two words—the Wikipedia page had the simple detail that out of eighty-seven ghats in Benaras, cremation happens on two, Harishchandra Ghat and Manikarnika Ghat. This information is also found on page 4 of Eck's book. I conducted this little experiment in order to determine how lazy Aslan and the CNN research team must have been—the show's promo claimed that *each* of the eighty-seven ghats has dead bodies burning every day and suggested that the whole city becomes a sort of a giant pyre.

The focus of the promo and indeed the episode on Hinduism was on the *aghoris*—a sect of extremely reclusive monks among Hindus. So small is the number of aghoris—a few hundred, if that, among a billion Hindus—that most Hindus have never really even heard of, let alone met, an aghori. The aghoris believe that nothing is profane because all that exists in the universe exists in oneself to some degree. *Believer* showed Aslan supposedly eating a piece of charred flesh with an aghori—with CNN flashing a CANNIBAL banner—and being offered urine to drink. There was a strange dichotomy in the use of language—the show's promo insisted that the ashes of the dead are "dumped" in the river rather than "immersed," which is the natural phrase that every Hindu, and certainly every religious scholar, would use. Clearly Aslan was not unfamiliar with the word—in one promo he talks about *immersing* himself in various religious practices for the sake of the camera.

It was not clear how much immersing Aslan had done but Eck, after fifteen years of engaging with Hinduism and indeed *immersing* herself in the study of the city of Benaras, noted on the same page 4 that "the cremation grounds are holy ground, for death in Kashi is acclaimed by the tradition as a great blessing. . . . Kashi is said to be the city of Shiva (the most eminent god in the Hindu trinity), founded at the dawn of civilization."[2] Clearly, not the City of the Dead.

Without even the slightest sense of irony, CNN ran these promos and the show days after a Hindu man in the United States was murdered by a man shouting racial slurs.

From the moment Aslan and CNN started tweeting promos of the show, there was uproar in many parts of the world. In America, congresswoman Tulsi Gabbard of the Democratic Party sent out a series of eleven tweets, where she said that she was "very disturbed that CNN is using its power and influence to increase people's misunderstanding and fear of Hinduism."[3]

Gabbard accused Aslan of trying to find "sensationalist and absurd ways to portray Hinduism."[4] She wrote:

> Aslan and CNN didn't just throw a harsh light on a sect of wandering ascetics to create shocking visuals—as if touring a zoo—but repeated false stereotypes about caste, karma, and reincarnation that Hindus have been combating tirelessly. CNN promotional materials and trailers that included a scene showing a group of Hindus under a caption "CANNIBALS" perpetuated bizarre and ugly impressions of Hindus and their religion. CNN knows well that sensational, even false reporting about religions only fosters ignorance that can lead to terrible consequences. Hindus are reeling after witnessing terrible hate crimes in the last few weeks.[5]

Vamsee Juluri, media studies scholar, asked Aslan a simple question through an essay in the *Huffington Post*:

> Would anyone in their right mind, or with a kind heart, have done a kitschy and voyeuristic program about an obscure and violent cult of Muslims on CNN in the years after 9/11? Why was Reza Aslan, a

pleasant and articulate professor, welcomed as the face of Muslims in
America on national TV and not some obscure hooded figure burning with fundamentalist zeal and violence?[6]

Before this book went to print, there had been no clear answer to
this question. However Aslan claimed in a tweet that his TV crew had
been the first to shoot at the cremation ghats. This was immediately
called out as false by two senior journalists in India—Yale World Fellow
Rahul Pandita and *Washington Post* columnist Barkha Dutt.

Meanwhile, in their dialogue on the subject with Aslan, the Hindu
American Foundation (HAF) asked why Aslan's series did not feature
any Muslim sects (there were some Christian sects featured apart from
the controversial episode on Hinduism). Aslan said no insurer could be
found for an episode on an Islamic sect.

HAF also noted that, according to the Pew Religious Knowledge
Survey 2013, only 36 percent of Americans could answer a "single question about Hinduism."[7] In such an atmosphere, "CNN is perpetuat-
ing . . . a very racist, colonial era discourse of dehumanization and even
demonization," wrote Juluri.[8]

It seems like the right time to publish a book on Hinduism in America from the point of view of those billion Hindus who don't really eat
human flesh or drink pee.

✿ ✿ ✿

When I was in school in Calcutta, from about the age of three until I
graduated at eighteen, I attended chapel service every morning. There
was no choice in the matter. I attended the Assembly of God Church
School. It was—still is—what you would call an American evangelical
Protestant school.

In a city of prestigious Anglo-Christian schools, many of them Catholic, tracing their history all the way back to the British Raj, my Protestant school was barely a few decades old. But what it lacked in history, it
tried to make up in two regards: charity dollars from America and
Canada, which helped it build not only some of the finest facilities in

Calcutta (brimming laboratories, beautiful basketball courts, and even its own hospital—one of the best at that time in the city); and it took its proselytizing seriously.

The Assembly of God Church School was founded by Reverend Mark Buntain and Mrs. Huldah Buntain. By the time I was old enough to have memories of them, Mark Buntain had died. But I remember Mrs. Buntain vividly. Meeting her was my first encounter with what I later learned was an American accent. When I first saw her, she was already in her sixties—a small woman with auburn hair and oversized tinted spectacles, draped in austerely cut single-tone satin dresses that were often in striking purple, brilliant blue, and sometimes coral colors. She was the first woman I had seen who wore a perfect string of pearls.

Mrs. Buntain, whenever she was in town, addressed us at chapel service. Often dwarfed by the pulpit, she resorted to using her voice to throw challenges at us. Were we sinning all the time? What would happen to those of us that sinned? Were we heading to hell? Why didn't we choose "God's love" and heaven? From my hard wooden bench in the cavernous school chapel with its burgundy leather-bound King James Bible in front of each seat, Mrs. Buntain seemed at once remote and enveloping. She spoke with the "trough-and-crest modulation" of North American television preachers. One moment she was whispering with the solemn power of God, the next she was invoking the sound and fury of the Almighty.

God, she told us, had performed miracles for her. Mrs. Buntain and her husband had arrived with few resources in Calcutta, and yet had been able to execute their ambitious mission. Jesus Christ, she said, was willing and ready to do miracles for us—each one of us. We believed her. At least my parents certainly did. After all, if it had not been for the Buntains, what would the status of my English-language school education be?

My father had neither the clout nor the money to enroll me into the old elite Catholic schools of Calcutta so with the arrival of the Buntains' relatively new English-medium school, my parents didn't bother much about the rest. The aggressive Protestant Pentecostal worldview meant little to them—or to me—except that it had opened the doors to a much-coveted English language education for me. This was Calcutta, the first city of the British Raj, and even in the 1980s when I entered school—three decades after the last of the white sahibs had left India— it was still a city that valued the English language.

Additionally Calcutta was discovering that English, when spoken by Americans, could often hint at an altogether different and greater sense of prosperity. Yet Mrs. Buntain, or Huldah, and her husband, the late Reverend Mark Buntain, were actually from Canada. Mark Buntain's father had been a pastor at a church in Winnipeg before he moved to Toronto and became the general superintendent of the Assemblies of God in Canada. Huldah's grandfather had preached at a church in Vancouver and her great-grandfather had been a Presbyterian minister in England. Long before she came to pestilential Calcutta, Huldah had known the East. Her parents had been missionaries in Japan, but after her grandfather died, her father returned to Vancouver to fill his preacher shoes. In 1954, barely in their thirties, Mark and Huldah and their infant daughter left Vancouver and traveled to New York. From there they took three ships and finally a barge to reach Calcutta after three long months for a stay intended to last only a year.

"When we docked in this city, the poverty . . . oh, the poverty," Huldah Buntain used to remind us. "I told Mark, 'What on earth can we do here? We have nothing, we are so young.'" And he used to tell me, "We can't, but God can."

Everyone has heard the legend of Mother Teresa but the story of the Buntains, dear friends of the saintly nun from Albania, is little known. Few are aware that until she died in 1997, some of the key doctors treating Mother Teresa were from the 173-bed multispecialty hospital that the Buntains had built on Park Street, the Fifth Avenue of Calcutta.

In the heart of a street where, even today, the rich of Calcutta come to play, where Christmas and New Year celebrations ring through the night, a sniff away from the quintessential English tea house Flurys, the Buntains built the city's most modern church.

When they started construction in the 1950s, it was the first new church the city had seen in perhaps a hundred years, and the Assembly of God Church School was one of the biggest coeducational schools in Calcutta, where the best schools had always been single-gender twin institutions: La Martiniere for Boys and La Martiniere for Girls, St. Xavier's and Loreto House, St. James' and Pratt Memorial. The Buntains and Mother Teresa had approached Calcutta's searing poverty almost from opposite ends—Teresa, through sheer will power and empathy, and the Buntains, in an almost entrepreneurial way, by building public institutions. One of her last memories of Mother Teresa, Huldah Buntain used to say, was of the saintly nun holding her hand and expounding: "When you help the poor, You. Do. It. Unto. Christ.—and hold up a finger for each word, and at the end you close it and it becomes a fist, strong and powerful in the aid of your mission." When Mother Teresa was dying, yet would not move to their six-floor charitable hospital, Mrs. Buntain helped build a treatment room at the house where Mother Teresa lived. Dr. Alfred Woodward, Mother Teresa's long-time doctor, was from the hospital built by the Buntains.

After they established the school and the hospital, the Buntains started daily free food distribution for thousands of the city's beggars, homeless, and shantytown poor.

By the time Mark Buntain died in 1989, the couple had created an Assemblies of God network in India of more than one hundred schools and seven hundred churches, a feeding program for twenty-five thousand people every day, and a hospital that treats more than two million each year—eight hundred thousand of them for free.

I have no memory of Mark Buntain, but his wife gave me my first bragging rights to a unique "foreign" connection. In a city steeped in colonial tradition, Mrs. Buntain was the next generation of aspiration. She came from "America." We middle-class, provincial schoolchildren didn't really understand the distinction between America and Canada at that time; it was all USA to us. We had never been abroad; neither had our parents.

Around the time I was born in 1979, Calcutta had begun to change. The Raj had not been forgotten, evident in its fragile clubs, as resilient as leaves held between pages of a book, that still insisted on gentlemen dressing for dinner—but on the streets the smell of a Communist revolution had begun to rise. Education was divided between the old pedigreed schools attended by the sons and daughters of the city's elite and Bengali-language schools for the rest; I wasn't eligible for the first, and there was no chance my parents would have been happy with the second. (A Bengali education suggested no future in those days and holds precious little opportunity even today.)

The Americans of the Assembly of God Church School (AGCS) shook up this status quo of distinction. In what I later learned to appreciate as the disrupting power of American money, it unsettled the pedagogical hierarchy of Calcutta. We at AGCS may not have possessed hundred-year-old school buildings, but we had Bose speakers in our chapel and the best American computers, the biggest Christmas tree, and the most lavish Christmas concert every year. When the first cola fountains came to Calcutta, my school got them first, adding to my stock of bragging rights. While the other top Anglicized schools competed in colonial snootiness, we disrupted the game. We were Americanized.

The intense chapel services were very much part of the experience as well.

During mass each day, different pastors solemnly walked up and stood on the large stage before us, holding fat Bibles full of post-it notes. Behind the wooden pulpit, which had a looming metal cross attached to the front, there was a wall-to-floor wooden cross that also formed the backdrop of the stage. The pastors would tell us stories from the Bible and the moral lessons those stories held. To begin with, I suppose one merely treated these stories as an extension of the imaginary universe one already knew from the great epics *Mahabharata*, *Ramayana*, and *Panchatantra*, and from the Bengali *Thakurmar Jhuli*, a much-loved set of children's tales. There were giants and heroes with swords flashing in them. The young David with a sling before Goliath, the hair of Samson that was the secret to his magical strength, Jesus miraculously multiplying bread and fish—it all seemed familiar. What we did not understand for many years was the deeper message. We did not comprehend that something else was being said to us, something that held these stories of magic as not stories of magic at all; lost in the prestidigitation, we missed the sleight of hand. That there was a hierarchy was lost on us—that our legends were lesser than their tales never occurred to us. Our inability to comprehend was also a reflection of our environment. No one had told us that these differences existed. We had neither seen nor heard conversations about ours and theirs. We assumed common ownership to fables and learned only later that even fables need to establish early their pole position. It had not occurred to us, at least not to me, that myths could war between themselves. It was at the question of sin that the light broke in.

Often the issue of sin was visited: what was sin, how one was and became a sinner, and what one could do to become sin-free. One of the main impressions of these long sessions was the idea that to not believe in Jesus was to be a sinner; to not "accept Jesus in your life" was to live a life of immorality that would certainly lead to hell. To deny the "one, true God" was blasphemy.

I must have been around twelve or thirteen years old when it first occurred to me that the whole idea of sin was a bit curious. The eureka moment came during a particularly fervent sermon just before the *Durga Puja* holidays—the ten-day break when the entire city of Calcutta fills with festivity, and gigantic idols of the goddess Durga are worshipped with fervor. That day, a pastor zealously told us that the Hindu practice of praying to gods and goddesses was false and heathen-like and would eventually bring forth greater sin. Only accepting Christ as "your personal savior" could save us, Mrs. Buntain had said. I remember giggling—it spilled out suddenly and without intent. Immediately, fear leaped in. I looked around—had a teacher noticed? Thankfully no, and so I permitted myself another grin; it seemed comical to me that after hearing such raucous exhortations against idol worship, we would merrily slip into a long, boisterous holiday of idol-worship excess.

It was also the first time I really thought about my faith. I was born Hindu. My parents are Hindu. So were my grandparents and their parents. As far back as anyone has ever checked, we have always been Hindu. But what did that mean? What did it mean to be Hindu? I had never asked my parents but had unquestioningly accepted that since they were Hindu, I must be Hindu too.

My parents and grandparents were closely associated with the Ramakrishna Math and Mission, which worked to propagate the worship methods and teachings of one of the last great seers of Hinduism, the unlettered nineteenth-century mystic Ramakrishna Paramhansa and his brilliant chief pupil, Swami Vivekananda, the man who won over America in 1893 with stirring speeches at the Parliament of the World's Religions in Chicago. In fact, words from Vivekananda's very first speech seem particularly topical today in America where calls to build a wall against immigrants and for refugee bans rend the air. On September 11, 1893 (ironically, another 9/11), the monk said:

> I am proud to belong to a nation which has sheltered the persecuted and the refugees of all religions and all nations of the earth. I am proud to tell you that we have gathered in our bosom the purest remnant of the Israelites, who came to Southern India and took refuge with us in the very year in which their holy temple was shattered to pieces by Roman tyranny. I am proud to belong to the religion which has sheltered and is still fostering the remnant of the grand Zoroastrian nation. I will quote to you, brethren, a few lines from a hymn which I remember to have repeated from my earliest boyhood, which is every day repeated by millions of human beings: "As the different streams having their sources in different places all mingle their water in the sea, so, O Lord, the different paths which men take through different tendencies, various though they appear, crooked or straight, all lead to Thee."[9]

The devotion of my parents to Vivekananda and the Ramakrishna Mission meant that they were often present at various branches of Hindu order to attend prayers and listen to and sometimes participate in the singing of hymns in Sanskrit, the ancient language of the great

Indian epics like the *Ramayana* and *Mahabharata* and of the founding treatises of Hindu philosophy, the *Vedas*, the *Upanishads*, and the *Puranas*. But apart from these hymns and a few mantras at weddings, I don't remember ever having heard Sanskrit anywhere. Who knew that this too was part of my heritage?

Who told us that, in my culture, this language is considered to take all believers ever closer to God? One would have wanted to feel the sonorous ring of Sanskrit in the head, but there was no access, no instruction. Today, I feel that this neglect, this starvation, has kept me and many like me strangely anemic. We learned about the world, but what about home? When I realized this loss much later in life, as I was nearing thirty, it came upon me as a most melancholic thing—the loss of something very intimate I had not known I possessed. While they sang hymns, I wondered why Sanskrit, once important to us as a civilization, was increasingly lost to us. After conducting a little research, I realized that what we had forgotten was pointed out by a NASA scientist in 1985. In *Artificial Intelligence* magazine, Rick Briggs published a paper entitled "Knowledge Representation in Sanskrit and Artificial Intelligence."[10] In this work, Briggs wrote,

> It is interesting . . . why the Indians found it worthwhile to pursue studies into unambiguous coding of natural languages into semantic elements. It is tempting to think of them as computer scientists without the hardware, but a possible explanation is that a search for clear, unambiguous understanding is inherent in the human being. Let us not forget that among the great accomplishments of the Indian thinkers was the invention of zero, and of the binary number system a thousand years before the West reinvented them. Their analysis of language casts doubt on the humanistic distinction between natural and artificial intelligence.

Among those around me, however, I did not see many people who thought of Sanskrit and artificial intelligence in relation to one another.

I often joined my parents at the hymn sessions at various branches of the Ramakrishna Mission. What seemed most attractive to me at that time was the cleanliness and quietude in these temples that, unlike most other Hindu temples, were almost always calm and reticent, publicity- and hyperbole-shy—except of course when the hymns were being sung. Even then, the music was sonorous, not cacophonous.

Paramhansa, during his mystical explorations, had studied with a Muslim *maulvi* and a Christian priest; and Vivekananda admired the teachings of Christ and the Buddha (whom he often spoke of as "the perfect man"). The Ramakrishna Math and Mission, then, accepted all faiths as being equally relevant paths to God, a thought summed up in Paramhansa's famous teaching, *"joto mot, toto poth"* or in other words, as many views as there are among men, there are ways to reach God.

Apart from their work with the Ramakrishna Math and Mission, my parents, like other Bengali Hindus, celebrated various festivals, including an elaborate Janmashtami to celebrate the birth of Krishna—one of the main avatars of Vishnu, the "preserver" in the Hindu trinity of Brahma-Vishnu-Shiva. As a schoolboy, all of these festivals only meant holidays and good food to me until that one day at chapel service when I began to wonder what being Hindu really meant to me—not to my parents, but to me, personally.

In a sense, I have been writing this book ever since. It has taken me a very long time, nearly two decades, to try to understand what my faith—which I share with a billion others—really translates into when interpreting everyday dilemmas. What was the relevance of God, it seems apt to ask once again, in a world being made unrecognizable by human intelligence, where today's magic is rapidly transforming into tomorrow's gadgets? In other words, what on earth does it really mean to be Hindu?

I prepared for years by reading ideas, interpretations, and evolutions of the principal tenets of the faith, but by the time I started writing this book, all the notes seemed inadequate and the words would not come. I realized that research was not enough; in order to write this book, I would need to question my own beliefs. Only by questioning my private vulnerabilities could I address what I thought, or felt, about my faith. As important as it was to me to understand what being Hindu meant theologically, it seemed even more urgent to discover what it meant to me personally. I turned to a man I usually turn to in moments of confusion—Vivekananda.

Vivekananda was a proponent of the *Vedanta*, a word often used to describe the core philosophies of the Vedas and other allied texts together; these are the most ancient spiritual texts known to man, the first of which were written, by some estimates, in 1700 BCE or more than 1700 years before Christ walked this earth. (It must be added here that different historians have given different timelines to the composition of the first Veda, anywhere between 1700 to 1200 BCE.) But the Vedanta is not confined to one book or even a few books. It is often used to describe the sum total of the whole body of Vedic and Upanishadic literature, and commentary on that literature, which stretches from the obscuring mists of ancient mankind right up to the present day. This makes the Vedanta unique in a way that is sometimes difficult to grasp entirely. The point is that the Vedanta and its teachings are not finite or time-bound. Even today, the arrival of a true mystic could further evolve the nuances of the Vedanta's teachings. While technically the Vedanta represents one of several schools of Indian philosophical and spiritual thought—indeed the Vedanta itself has multiple iterations—to me, as a common practitioner, the Vedanta holds many sublime ideas which deal directly with the everyday practice of Hinduism. This book is not an academic exploration of the subtle nuances between various philosophical schools of Hindu thought; rather, it is a collection of lessons, such as they are, from the experiences of one practitioner trying to make sense of what the dialectic means in real life and in the day-to-day practice of a faith.

In this regard, the Vedanta is perhaps one of the only truly *alive* spiritual texts the world has ever known, a text unfettered by time and unrestricted by historicity. It lives and transforms unremittingly because its fundamental core beliefs are held to be timelessly true.

What are these beliefs—this *sanatana dharma* or eternal law—that claim to live on unaltered and yet are constantly absorbing, assimilating, adjusting for several millennia? The English novelist and Vedanta explorer Christopher Isherwood wrote a distillation titled *What is Vedanta?*[11] on this question, which I think is apt. He says, "Reduced to its elements, Vedanta philosophy consists of three propositions. First, man's real nature is divine. Second, the aim of human life is to realize this divine nature. And finally, all religions are essentially in agreement." Each of these propositions, or truths if you will, and the exploration of what they really mean in everyday life—in my life and in the lives of millions of other Hindus—is what propelled me to write this book.

The world of theology is divided into the Abrahamic and non-Abrahamic faiths or, to simplify, faiths that have one guiding book and those that do not. To illustrate, the three great monotheistic faiths—Christianity, Islam, and Judaism—each uphold that there is only one true path to God and share the character of Abraham as a founding father; they are also religions that abide by the principles stated in one guiding book. With the exception of Sikhism, this is not true for religions that emerged from the Indian subcontinent such as Hinduism, Buddhism, and Jainism and those from other Eastern faiths such as Taoism and Shintoism.

But what does all this theory really mean in everyday life? As I entered adulthood in India, one thing became increasingly and starkly apparent to me. After the terrorist-hijacked planes crashed into the twin towers in New York on September 11, 2001, the global conversation about faith narrowed to swirl around what it means to be Muslim, and in contrast, what it means to be Christian.

Samuel Huntington, father of the "Clash of Civilizations" theory, was not only a renowned conservative political scientist but was also the cofounder and the coeditor of the influential *Foreign Policy* magazine and so, I often think, it is not surprising that Islam versus Christianity was a theme long before it became breaking news. The "Clash of Civilizations" theory argues that religious and cultural beliefs will be the main source of strife and violence in the post–Cold War world. With Islamist terror attacks mushrooming around the world, and a backlash against Muslim migration across Europe and America banning the entry of people from some Muslim majority countries, this scenario seems inevitable to many people.

I began thinking about my book in the aftermath of 9/11. As a young journalist, when I saw the twin towers come crashing down on the TV set, I knew my own world and the world in general would never be the same; I remember asking myself, where does all this leave us, the Hindus? Which side, if any, are we on? (I hoped that we would promote peace among all faiths, but in the middle of conflict, was that too simplistic a deduction? I fervently hoped—and continue to hope—not.) It was impossible for me, as an Indian, not to see that my own country—with its long and varied history of invasion, occupation, and unequal assimilation as well as violent partition between Hindus and Muslims, with smaller skirmishes between Hindus and Christians or Sikhs—was continually vulnerable to such fissures. Religion, I had often heard, was the soul of India. But history also makes clear that that soul can easily be wounded, and that dormant resentments can quickly and volcanically come alive. My own grandparents fled what is today Bangladesh during the partition of the Indian subcontinent at independence from British colonial rule in 1947.

This subject is particularly complicated and dangerously prickly in a country whose history is so diverse and complex. Christianity came to India around the sixth century, some believe with the Apostle Thomas, who visited the southern state of Kerala. At last count, around 24 million (2.3 percent) of Indians were Christians. Islam, which first appeared in India around the seventh century CE, really took root with the Turkish invasions around the twelfth century. Islam's high noon, of course, was the three-hundred-year-long Mughal Empire which, at its zenith, stretched from Samarkand in Central Asia all the way up to the Deccan Plateau in southern India. Today, nearly 180 million Indians, or more than 14 percent of the population, are Muslims.

Just under 80 percent of India remains Hindu—evidence of a resilient, and sometimes bewilderingly, polytheistic faith with a legendary 330 million gods and goddesses—which neither Christianity (with a hundred-year British Raj and, before it, Jesuits from Spain, Italy, and,

later, France and Portugal) nor centuries-long Islamic rule could subdue or convert. In fact, Hinduism assimilated both those faiths in the
country, allowing the flourishing of Sufism, a relatively liberal and tolerant subsect of Islam that holds some ideas similar to Hinduism, including patron saints or *pir*, and numerous holy shrines (*dargahs*) where the
faithful gather. None of these are incorporated into the orthodox, puritanical ideas of the Islam of Arabia where the faith was born. As I
finished editing the American edition of this book, I further questioned
what issues will dominate and determine the world of tomorrow. Everywhere I look as a journalist, the answers seem to throw two broad
answers at me: Conflict between Islam and Christianity (the latter
sometimes referred to as "the West"); and the rise of Asia.

In all the current discussions about China's growing influence and
Japan's prosperity, there seems to be a far greater global awareness
about Buddhism—if not about Confucianism, Shintoism, Taoism, and
so on. Much of this is due (to the permanent irritation of China) to the
expansive efforts around the world of His Holiness the Dalai Lama and
his many confidants and disciples, including those in Hollywood.

But the mainstream understanding of Hinduism still seems superfi-
cial, perfunctory, and reduced to caricatures and platitudes. For instance, Hindus are one of the fastest-growing communities in the United States, but a poll by the Pew Global Research Center in 2014
showed that Americans had distinctly mixed feelings about Hindus,
with a positive perception ranking of barely fifty out of a maximum of a
hundred. This statistic was just ten points above Muslims in spite of the
fact that Hindus have been consistently one of the most integrated
immigrant communities in America with little history of conflict. There
have been no American troops in "Hindu lands" and no Hindu suicide
bombers, no discussions of drones and no comparisons of good Hindu/
bad Hindu, no incidents of terror and no suggestions of an occupation
dressed up as democracy. Hindus in America have mostly been spoken
of in terms of their involvement in information technology, finance,
mathematics, and the sciences—more attention is given to "geekiness"
than to grievances. Yet, some prejudices persist. Those who profess a

faith that sees itself as the vessel of eternal truth have been caricaturized as worshippers of cows, monkeys, and snakes. Hinduism has seen its virtues isolated and commercialized, its vices red-flagged.

Helpfully, the survey also pointed out that although yoga is soaring in popularity amongst cosmopolitan Americans, few connect it to Hinduism, although in reality it is an intrinsic act of the faith first practiced by the ancient sages. Its noncanonical, non-base text, polymath approach often results in Hinduism being reduced to caricatures—as the survey also hinted—or to the worship of cows and the social stigmas of caste. One would think that a faith that accepted all religions and expressions of faith as equally valid 1,700 years ago would be the most studied and treasured in a world of sectarian religious strife—but clearly that is not true.

Millions of Indians went about their daily rituals in keeping with the path of Hinduism they followed, but I noticed a growing and persistent lack of enthusiasm, a hesitance, about declaring themselves Hindu, especially among youth in general, but among my colleagues and friends as well. I felt it too. As one of my closest friends complained, "It is much clearer for Muslims and Christians—you read the book and you make up your mind. It is so much more complicated for us; there is just too much ambiguity and too many layers."

Curiously, since the core beliefs of Hinduism leave almost all decisions to the individual—after all, even atheists can technically be Hindu—more and more people felt their understanding to be hazy and undefined. Instead of seeing the undefined as liberating, we had begun to view it as faith unresolved and unsubstantial. It was almost as if we were asking that the responsibility of spiritual choice to be taken away from us, or at least not left to us to this vague extent.

While the world waited for the Indian elephant to rise (or dance, as some put it), apparently few really understood the nuances of the civilizational beliefs of most Indians. In fact, we Hindus, as well as Indians belonging to other faiths, didn't really understand them either, or we had forgotten.

While writing this book and in my work as a journalist, I often hear
things like, "Hinduism is the bulwark against Islamofascism in India" or
"the Buddha will find the common ground amongst the great Asian
civilizations—China, Japan, and India. After all, the Buddha came from
India." In the meantime the rise of the Bharatiya Janata Party (BJP),
often unflatteringly described as the "Hindu Right," and the grand victory of prime minister Narendra Modi in 2014, has brought about a
spate of new writing—some hysterical and fear-mongering, some faintly
ridiculous—about impending doom in religious harmony in India, or
even genocide. Extreme statements from some elements of fundamentalist fringe Hindu organizations in India have also caused problems.
From an inherently come-as-you-are pacifist faith, Hinduism seems to
have acquired, in many minds, an unprecedented ultra-militant edge. A
few attacks by fringe groups of Hindu hardliners on Muslims and other
minority groups—especially with regard to the issue of cow slaughter
and the sale and consumption of beef, considered abominable by most
Hindus and illegal in most parts of India—have also sullied the atmosphere. Even though India is one of the biggest exporters of buffalo
meat in the world, killing and eating the meat of cows remains a taboo
for most Hindus, and is banned by law in most of India. The authors of
the modern Indian nation-state advised against cow slaughter, keeping
in mind popular sentiments in the Indian constitution as well. This is
not new. While there is some evidence that ancient Hindus may have
eaten cow meat, beef eating has been repugnant to Hindus for hundreds of years. In the medieval period, the Muslim emperor Babur,
who started the Mughal dynasty in India, warned his son in a letter not
to allow the slaughter of cows as it would turn his (mostly) Hindu
subjects against the ruler. But even so, the attacks, vile and immoral,
shocked me; in a sense it made my resolution to write this book even
more steadfast. It seems it is the right time for a believing, modern
Hindu to speak up and assert the values he has imbibed.

Amid the frenzy, what is missing is a studious attempt to understand
what is really happening to a billion-strong faith. There is little understanding on how Hindus see themselves and their role in this world.

What are the unique virtues, if any, that India's Hindu civilization has to offer in the twenty-first century? What are the values, systems, and ideas that this civilization can hold forth for the future? In centuries of assimilation and alteration, how has Hinduism's own perception of itself transformed, and how does it see itself and the world today? If India, where a majority of the people are Hindus—though the state is constitutionally secular—is to be a determining pillar of global polity in the twenty-first century, answers to these questions are critical, not just for Indians but also for the world. A nuanced understanding of what it means to be Hindu and how to handle Hindu identity in the twenty-first century is critical to India's comprehension of its role in the modern world.

Progress cannot occur unless Hindus first understand who they are, where they come from, and where they are going; we need to comprehensively and cohesively explain what the worldview of our faith, so often intertwined in our moral and geopolitical belief systems, really is. There has been a myth in India that Hindus do not, ever, place their moral and political superstructures and points of view in the philosophies of their faith. This is untrue, and one of the people who truly understood this was Gandhi. His infusion of Hindu belief systems, idioms, iconography, and commitment to plurality—which came directly from the core principle of the *Rig Veda*: *e kam sat vipra bahudha vadanti* (truth is one, the sages manifest it variously)—lifted the moribund Indian National Congress from a tepid, elite debating society to a fervent national movement. At every step of his life, in every decision, Gandhi declared that his guiding principles came from the *Bhagavad Gita*, the moral lessons embedded in the epic *Mahabharata* given by the god Krishna to the warrior Arjun on the meaning of life, God-realization, and the essence of conflict on the battlefield of Kurukshetra. Gandhi called the book his spiritual dictionary.

So unapologetically sanguine was Gandhi on his (and his faith's) commitment to plurality—and especially in India's case, the deep and historic bonds between Hindus and Muslims—that he was murdered by a Hindu bigot who believed that Gandhi had orchestrated the partition of India at the end of the British Raj to create Pakistan, a homeland for Muslims, even though around 14 percent of India remained Muslim and, therefore, was never in correlation a homeland for Hindus alone. Gandhi's faith in this communal cohesion, even after the partition brought with it a massacre of a million people in sectarian riots—largely between Hindus and Muslims—and his complete disregard for his own personal safety finally felled him to an assassin's bullet in 1948, barely a year after independence.

And here is the unique twist that only the inherent, genetic plurality of Hinduism could have given to this tale: Gandhi's murderer Nathuram Godse proclaimed his own belief in plurality and the right of Hindus and Muslims to coexist in India! In his infamous speech in court, before he was tried and hung—a fact that was banned from publication in India until 1968—Godse declared that he had killed Gandhi because of the division of the land between the two countries, and because he believed Gandhi had allowed it to make the Muslims happy. But it is almost never noted that Godse did not make the claim, nor express a desire, that Hindus and Muslims should not share a homeland after the British left India. As an avowed "Hindu nationalist" as he is often declared to be, it is curious that he made no demand for the creation of a Hindu nation as one might expect given that death-row statements on behalf of a cause generally receive wide attention. On the contrary, Godse said in court, "In my speeches and writings, I have always advocated that the religious and communal consideration should be entirely eschewed in the public affairs of the country; at elections, inside and outside the legislatures and in the making and unmaking of Cabinets. I have throughout stood for a secular state with joint electorates. To my mind this is the only sensible thing to do."[12]

Here are two men doomed by the nefarious force of history to be martyr and assassin, and thus to define the soul of an old yet modern nation. Both of them declare their faith in plurality: Gandhi through his martyrdom and Godse even through his last words when he could have cried out for a Hindu nation if he had so wished. Both were never anything but Hindu. The story of Gandhi's death (and life) is so ubiqui-

tous that it has become, in some ways, almost stripped of deeper meaning by incessant mythologizing. But as I discovered and pondered on
this commonality, it threw me off guard. Here were the saint and the
sinner both vouching to the end for the plurality of Hinduism. I do not
wish to give the impression here that I am in any way making some sort
of moral equivalence between the opinions of Gandhi and Godse. What
I am trying to show is that even when it seems logical for Godse to
demand a Hindu-only state, somehow, through some astonishing mind
shift, he talks instead about a secular state. Here are two Hindus at the
two very extremes of an argument, but somehow their faith leads them
to say similar things—even when one kills the other. I am presenting
you, the reader, with this compelling scenario, and leaving you to decide what to make of it.

This book is not meant to be the final word in historical treatise
writing, and I am not a historian. Instead, it is an account of my personal journey in trying to understand what being Hindu means to me as
well as to many others I have met through my decade-long effort to
understand my faith. It is important to emphasize that while Hinduism
has many streams of thought and many philosophies, I have here described what appeals most to me—the Hinduism taught by Vivekananda, and before him, by Shankaracharya, said to have lived sometime
between the sixth and eighth century CE—whose works are the foundation of the *Advaita Vedanta* doctrine. This book does not in any way
claim to distill down all of Hindu thought. It is meant to be read as an
intimate journey of personal experience and not academic theorizing.
The core lesson I have learned from my experience of Hindu thought is
that, at its very heart, Hindu is concerned with understanding the truth,
and the truth, one is told, lies not in the world but in one's self. In their
exhaustive series on the history of philosophy, Peter Adamson and Jonardon Ganeri quote from the *Brihadaranyaka Upanishad*: "It is one's
self that one should see and hear and upon which one should reflect
and contemplate for it is by seeing and hearing one's self and by reflecting and concentrating on one's self one gains the knowledge of this

whole world."[13] This simple but limitless idea is the bedrock on which my experience of Hinduism stands.

Hinduism, as I see it, teaches that there are really only three questions that deserve answering—who am I, what do I want, and what is my purpose? And of these, the most important is: who am I? It is said that it takes a lifetime even to understand the questions properly, let alone to find the answers.

Perhaps to intellectually understand Hinduism is impossible—much like the Vedic description of the truth encapsulated in the expression *neti, neti* (not this, not this). The phrase suggests a philosophical line of inquiry where once you negate all that you can materially comprehend, that which remains is the truth, the Absolute, the Brahman. You can only fully comprehend the Absolute when, through spiritual evolution, you are one with it. (If I were already, of course I wouldn't be writing this book, you see.)

As I keep circling the question in my mind: what on earth does this mean in everyday life? I want to try to understand and, perhaps in the process of understanding, help to explain. If this exploration reveals some aspects of Hinduism and how it relates to the world, thereby helping someone else understand, I will naturally be delighted.

I

HOW TO WRITE ABOUT HINDUS

I was once asked: "Is it true that the Hindus believe in dancing gods?" A nearly naked dancing god—was that part of Hinduism? This was the question of a polite elderly gentleman who was a distinguished member of the Harvard Club in Manhattan where I was giving a talk. He was referring to the Nataraj statue, from CERN, the European Organization for Nuclear Research, which is home to the Large Hadron Collider, and was intrigued by its presence. We had a long conversation about the relevance of the dancing Shiva in which I tried to explain to him the philosophy of the Nataraj: the representation of the constant chain of creation and destruction in the universe. As the art historian Ananda Coomaraswamy has also written, the dance represents the god Shiva's five activities—creation and evolution; preservation; destruction and further evolution; illusion and rest; and release, salvation, and grace.[1] What to most Western eyes is a wild-eyed image of a man—in a tiger skin, dancing dervish-like, drum in hand, his matted locks in a storm—is in reality the succinct representation of relentless creation and destruction, and the creation again of life itself. A fascinating belief system, yet packaged in caricature to audiences. Over the years that I have pondered writing this book, I have been fascinated by the many curious beliefs about Hinduism, some funny, some fantastical, almost all unrecognizable to practicing Hindus like me.

As I spoke to people, friends and strangers, around India and the world—on Delhi streets and Kolkata bookstores, in Mumbai restaurants and Bangalore clubs, waiting for the train at Notting Hill Gate station, in a village in Rajasthan, at a bar in Copenhagen, outside the Harvard Club in New York—wherever I could, I'd work a question or two about Hinduism into the conversation. The answers I received sometimes amused, sometimes perplexed me. Yoga was frequently mentioned (yet not much about the spiritual principles behind it), and I heard about cows and the caste system as well as the refrain "many gods and goddesses," but it seemed that the "color"—as we journalists say—more often than not obscured any understanding about the richness of the philosophies, some of the oldest, most evolved principles known to man. The caricatures, it seemed to me, had hardened into prejudices that blurred the core philosophies.

It occurred to me that knowledge about this multitudinous, multilateral faith—with its numerous sub-belief systems and also one great, foundational narrative—is almost impossible for most people outside the country (and indeed, even inside the country) to comprehend and communicate. In this specific context, most Hindus have experienced a simple unwavering quality in their faith, which has seen them through hundreds of years of Islamic and British rule, as well as hundreds of invasions. But ask most Hindus to explain the principles, history, and belief systems of their faith and they struggle. There is a reason why this is true. Conversion or proselytizing has never been core to the worldview of Hinduism in any shape or form, whereas these are essential practices in Islam and often in Christianity as well. Ask a Hindu if he or she knows of verses, scriptures, or active efforts to convince and convert—and the answer will mostly be no. The idea of proselytizing or spreading the faith by inducting more followers is not a characteristically Hindu way of thinking. The emphasis in Hinduism is on the personal, the private, and so the spread of the collective has less meaning. There are some Hindu groups like the Hare Krishna movement which actively seek "members," but this is not central in any way to the manner in which most Hindus access and address their faith. The lack of proselytizing zeal means that the average Hindu is far less articulate in distilling his or her vast polytheistic philosophical ideals than someone who practices a monotheistic faith. At an everyday level, I've observed, the Hindu relies not so much on scriptural texts but on life experiences. A Hindu usually finds it easier to describe his relationship with the divine, with the spiritual part of his life, than to explain the faith in its totality. Since the subtexts are so diverse (remember those 330 million gods and goddesses?), ordinary worshippers are often not able to identify and articulate the dominant themes of Hinduism. They can, however, talk about their personal, empirical faith.

In no way does this imply that there are not dominant or core themes and values embedded in Hindu literature and rituals; they are often deeply complex and nuanced theological ideas. What happens more often than not is that believers or practitioners, people like me for instance, tend to become obsessed with the rituals at the cost of understanding the philosophies. We will address some of these themes through the book, but for the moment, let us return to my initial discoveries of what many people think about Hinduism. For instance, I learned that some shared the point of view that the great Hindu epics—the *Mahabharata* and the *Ramayana*—were "fantasy stories," essentially fiction with no intrinsic historical value. Some even said that to confer any historicity to mythology is illiterate and idiotic. However, I disagree. I do not believe that every idea and thought in every so-called Hindu text should be accepted as the truth. That would go against the Hindu idea of relentless inquiry, that it is our duty to question everything before believing in it. But some have grains of truth.

Let us take an example from the lectures delivered by D. R. Bhandarkar, one of the finest Indian archaeologists of his day, on ancient Indian history (specifically the period between 650 and 325 BCE) at Calcutta University in February 1918.[2] In his exploration of antiquity, Bhandarkar constantly points out how references in the *Ramayana* and the *Mahabharata*, written as they were by men who attempted to capture the zeitgeists, help confirm many historical facts. I shall illustrate only three points from Bhandarkar's lectures as examples.

In one lecture, Bhandarkar talks about a Kshatriya (the warrior caste of the four primary Hindu castes) tribe called Bhoja. He confirms their existence from references in Kautilya's *Arthashastra*—which is the great ancient Indian socioeconomic treatise predating Florentine Niccolo Machiavelli's advice on statecraft, *The Prince*, by around 1,600 years—to the *Mahabharata* and the *Harivamsa*, one of the important appendices to the *Mahabharata*.

Then there is a reference to the Ikshvakus, a major ruling clan from the north of India. Bhandarkar confirms the presence of the Ikshvakus from three sources: first, inscriptions that have been discovered by archaeologists from the third century that talk about the reign of King Madhariputra Sri Virapurushadatta of the Ikshvaku family; second, from the *Ramayana* we know that Lord Rama—the hero of the text— was part of the Ikshvaku race; and finally, Buddhist texts tell us that so was the Buddha.

My final example from Bhandarkar's teachings has to do with the Brahmin sage, Agastya. Now, Agastya is mentioned in the *Ramayana* as among the first to have crossed the Vindhya mountains and is admitted by all Tamil grammarians as the founder of the Tamil language, the great Tamirmuni, or sage of the Tamils. Also, Bhandarkar points out that if you read Robert Caldwell's *Grammar of the Dravidian or South-Indian Family of Languages*, there is mention of a hill where Agastya retired after his work in bringing forth the Tamil language.[3] This hill, called Agastiar (Agastya's Hill) by local tradition and later adopted by the British, can still be found in the Tinnevelly district of Tamil Nadu, a state in southern India. The point is simply this: it is erroneous to suppose that myths and legends are not intertwined with history. What might be considered merely myth often has deep connections to real events and real people.

Bhandarkar's commentary is of prime importance, "I am not unaware that these are legends. It is however a mistake to suppose that legends teach us nothing historical."[4] This is exactly the point of revisiting ancient mythology from a historical perspective—to ensure that we make relevant connections between the myths and our everyday landscape so that the legends do not remain fantastic and far away. The purpose is not to prove that Rama was a historical figure per se but to show the connections between what we know as history and what we know as myth, and to examine how the two cross-pollinate to give us a sense of our national moorings. This reflexive relationship between history and mythology is exactly the point Lord Meghnad Desai, noted economist, historian, and British Labour Party peer, once made to me on the subject. He emphasized that the Bible had been studied for historical references as had *The Iliad* and *The Odyssey* in relation to Greek history.

The great Indian historian, Ramesh Chandra Majumdar, who edited the definitive eleven-volume *History and Culture of the Indian People*, talked about the importance of the work done by Frederick Eden Pargiter, a British expert on ancient India, "to reconstruct a continuous historical narrative from the data, particularly the royal genealogies, contained in the *Puranas* and the epics like *Mahabharata* and *Ramayana*" which Majumdar said "offer the only fair basis on which the ancient political history of India can be built up."[5] "Pargiter has at least successfully demonstrated that it is a mistake to regard such great historical figures like Puru, Mandhata, Nahusha, Yayati, Kartavirya, Arjun, etc., as mere fanciful and mythological, and any theory that gives them some sort of historical setting cannot but be regarded as of great value,"[6] Majumdar writes. The question here is simple but often not easy to absolutely answer—which parts of our myths and legends are intrinsically tied to history and which are not? I have felt that we in India, especially due to our long history of subjugation, have often been derisory and dismissive about our ancient achievements. This attitude probably also comes from a post-independence ethos wherein tradition is sometimes seen as archaic and redundant as the nation searches for a modern identity. Nehru famously called big dams the temples of modern India but, as we advanced along that line of thinking, did we somewhere develop a feeling that the only way to view temples is with intellectual disdain? Did we retain the sneer of our oppressors with regard to our own culture and science? Have we done enough to approach and embrace our heritage with confidence and without condescension?

All of these questions occurred to me when I heard the assertion that any talk of scholarship, especially in the sciences, in ancient India was fraudulent, and then something curious caught my eye. A mathematician of Indian origin, Manjul Bhargava, won the Fields Medal in 2014, one of the highest prizes for excellence in mathematics. One of Bhargava's greatest achievements was solving a two-hundred-year-old mathematical problem. How did he do it? Bhargava says he was able to accomplish this by reading old Sanskrit manuscripts that had been preserved by his grandfather, Purshottam Lal Bhargava, as head of the Sanskrit Department at the University of Rajasthan. In the library reserves he found the work of seventh-century Indian mathematician Brahmagupta and he realized, using Brahmagupta's work, that he could crack a problem unresolved for two centuries. Essentially, when two numbers which are both the sum of two perfect squares are multiplied together, the result is also the sum of two perfect squares. He found a generalization of this principle in Brahmagupta's work that helped him simplify the expansive composition law introduced by German Carl Friedrich Gauss in 1801.

Stumbling onto such examples in my research, where myth and history meet practical circumstances, is fascinating because so often I hear how most ancient Indian knowledge is, at best, dated and of little value today. I decided to dismantle and understand a few things about ancient Indian knowledge for myself. Further research revealed that Brahmagupta was one of the greatest mathematicians of all time, the first to introduce in India the concept of negative numbers and to spell out their rules of operation. His two seminal books are *Brāhmasphuṭasiddhānta* and *Khaṇḍakhādyaka*. The only reason Bhargava could access this text and theory was because of his grandfather's knowledge of the Sanskrit language and its texts.

While I was catching up on history, a controversy broke out about celebrating Sanskrit Week in India (some felt that celebrating Sanskrit Week and searching for the River Saraswati would offend followers of minority religions in India and make the country less secular); and a government-led search for the Saraswati River, whose trail had dried up and disappeared long ago, led to acerbic commentary, even though it was conducted by the highly reputable ISRO (the Indian Space Research Organisation, which made headlines in 2013 for launching the cheapest Mars mission in the world and again in 2017 for sending the largest number of satellites, 104, into space via a single rocket) and despite the fact that the river had also been rediscovered in 1855 by a French geographer, Louis Vivien de Saint Martin. The debate on Sanskrit prompted me to look up what others had to say with regard to this language of ancient Indian religious and social texts. To my surprise, I found that many of the well-known experts on Sanskrit, and even on Hinduism, are found in the West, especially in the United States. Since most theological documentation, especially the near-infinite variety found in the Hindu system, is intrinsically open to interpretation, conclusion(s) are highly dependent on the contextual lenses used. I realized that however scholarly they might be, some Western experts use Western idioms, ideologies, and theories to interpret Indian theology and philosophy, which might yield faulty explanations. Since India is producing few experts of its own who are experienced in the practice of the faith, some of these inaccurate notions tend to swiftly become regarded as "truth," not just by Westerners but by everyone. What ought to be a debate has leap-frogged into a monologue. At least in India, Sanskrit and ancient systems of knowledge have gathered a thick film of "colonial sneer" which many years of postcolonial history have struggled to remove. Ironically, I found that the early Orientalists were some of the last great champions of Indology. William Jones, one of the great Orientalists before the Bengal Renaissance (the nineteenth- to early twentieth-century social reform movement in the eastern Indian state of Bengal in India that saw a flowering of intellectual talent and the eradication of many forms of social discrimination), wrote that he found Sanskrit to be "more perfect than Greek, more copious than Latin, and more exquisitely refined than either."[7] Henry Colebrooke, another strikingly diligent Orientalist, discovered that Brahmagupta, and the

sixth-century astronomer Aryabhata, were some of the pioneers of algebra and arithmetic.

Comparing Aryabhata's work to that of the Hellenic Diophantus,
Colebrooke even concluded that the algebra of the Indians was more
distinguished than that of the Greeks. I began to ask—do we only
accept our own knowledge if it comes branded, interpreted, and neatly
labeled from the West, like our understanding of yoga? Was this that
old Indian servility rearing its ugly head again—a perpetuation of the
joke that we never consider anything we have or do to be good enough
unless the West says so? It seemed to me that the decolonization of our
minds could only begin if we start to consider that our history might be
what others did not write. As I looked around and read all that was
being written about India and often about Hinduism, I struggled to find
the right language to describe what I was feeling. Then I found a marvelous, cliché-shattering short essay by the African writer Binyavanga
Wainaina, "How To Write About Africa." Wainaina's contribution criti-
cally examines the Western gaze on Africa, while engaging with his own
identity as a Kenyan homosexual writer who rose from modest beginnings to become an author of renown, as well as the director of the
Chinua Achebe Centre for African Writers and Artists at Bard College.
This essay pointed out, all at once, the taboos and hypocrisies about
Africa embodied in spirited lines like, "Describe, in detail, naked
breasts . . . or mutilated genitals, or enhanced genitals. Or any kind of
genitals. And dead bodies. Or, better, naked dead bodies. . . . Remember, any work you submit in which people look filthy and miserable will
be referred to as the 'real Africa.'"[8] It painted, in harshly sarcastic
terms, the flawed language employed to box in and caricaturize descrip-
tions of Africa, especially by those in the West. It used the language of
the West to portray the deep-seated prejudices that Africa continues to
face. In 2007, it became clear that Wainaina was not just another talent
discovered in the Third World when he declined the Young Global
Leader award, which is presented to people who demonstrate a potential to contribute to shaping the future of the world. As a reply to the
nominating authority, he wrote a letter that acknowledged the tempta-

tion to attend the award ceremony, but placed it secondary to the point that he was trying to make. He wrote, "The problem here is that I am a writer. And although, like many, I go to sleep at night fantasizing about fame, fortune and credibility, the thing that is most valuable in my trade is to try, all the time, to keep myself loose, independent and creative . . . it would be an act of great fraudulence for me to accept the trite idea that I am 'going to significantly impact world affairs.'" Reading his essay was a moment of epiphany for me. I had found the guru of my voice. So I wrote an essay—sort of an ode to "How To Write About Africa"— which I called "How To Write About Hindus With A Left Hand." This short essay gave me the tone and verve of what I want to say in this book; it told me what I should leave out, and what I should keep. It taught me to fiercely focus on the issue at hand as I see it.

This is what I wrote:

> Always use the word "Hindu" as if you really meant to write "Hindoo" (colonial spelling used to suggest parody) but are too polite. Words like "dusk," "soul," "heterodox," "bourgeois," "traditional," "Orientalist," naturally, help. Subtitles may include the words "ancient," "plural," "civilization," "alternative," "sex." The last one is of the most vital significance. Without it, your book (article, essay) and Hinduism are doomed. Its soul will never be discovered.
>
> The pictures you use along with the writing can never have kind, well-adjusted, pleasantly God-fearing folk. They should have great matted hair. A bushy chest. A trident in the hand really helps. They can't wear too many clothes. It spoils the image of the warrior *sadhu*—the monk doth protest too much is a powerful tool. Don't treat it lightly. Or you can have a bespectacled, grouchy old man holding a grammatically incorrect banner. Looking angry.
>
> Make them stand on the right side of the frame of your image. That explains the number of times you will be writing right-wing. If they are helpful, they can even lean a little to the right. Preferably using the trident (carried as a weapon by the god Shiva, the Destroyer in the Hindu trinity; the other two are Brahma, the Creator, and Vishnu, the Preserver). Or the misspelled banner.

In your text, constantly refer to the vastness of Hinduism; use poly- a lot (it can be theistic, even gamy); put *heterogeneousness* in every other sentence, but essentially treat Hindus as one slightly off-centre whole. You will use the word *monolith*—it means one uniform entity. That's how you should treat Hinduism. Though you must not, ever, say so.

Always call Hinduism a "way of life." It's like saying "Open, Sesame." "Way of life" is like the sari. It hides a multitude of sins. All the greedy excess and binge drinking neatly hidden behind its pleated folds. Once you declare "way of life" you are free to say anything.

Begin by writing that you love all gods and goddesses. The Hindus have many of these. So there are many books (articles, essays) to be written. But nowhere have you mentioned snake charmers or elephants. So your work is not about hunting down the exotic. It is scholarship. Oh, sorry, you did mention an elephant god. You said his trunk is the penis. Or his penis is the trunk. One can't be entirely sure but there is some cock (and bull) there. It is, after all, a way of life.

Move quickly to sex. Too much meditation and spirituality becomes boring. Or like yoga. And why would someone read you for that? Bikram does it better. George, you know? Clooney? Him, and Madonna, and Lady Gaga—they all go there. One client for every generation.

Taboo subjects—Hindus quietly praying. Hindus writing philosophy. Or theology. Hindus going about their daily lives; or Hindus not beating women, not raping women, not showing penis, or breasts or vagina.

One of the biggest points of your book must always be that there are no rules in Hinduism. You must profess great love for Hinduism at the beginning of the book. It could begin by talking about your mother showing you the colors of India. From your mother's cheap batik scarf to loving Hindu texts is a small distance—which your book can easily cover.

Describe in detail the colors of India. The colors of mud (on Hindus who are naked), the colors of the trees (which are standing up, you know, like penises), the color of the sky (blue, like what the woman feels like after coitus sometimes), the color of the festivals (red, like menstrual blood)—say that you love all these colors. Especially if there are naked people in them. And that all those colors are colors of copulation for the Hindus.

Always subtly hint that while you have read and mastered all Hindu texts, there is actually nothing called Hinduism. This must be the great consistent revelation of your book. It is also great preparation just in case someone spots your errors and takes you to court.

The more you write that you love the openness in Hinduism, the better it is for you. Because if nothing exists, and there are no rules, no facts, no realities and no texts—if there is no Hinduism—then you can write what you want. And anything you write will make you a scholar.

So in this nothing-exists-ness, you can cleverly make everything into those three vital truths about the Hindus—naked, vagina, and penis.

Try never to say anything good about any Hindu god or goddess (unless you are saying something about their penis or vagina or both). But always say that all the villains in Hindu stories were actually the good guys. Only misunderstood and misrepresented—like the National Rifle Association, or the Taliban. Never talk about the penis or vagina of the villains. Never describe them as naked. But the heroes must always be sex crazy, lustful and raping. Only gods rape—demons don't. That's another great revelation you will discover during your research.

Never get your book reviewed by any practicing Hindu.

Your book needs a cover where many gods and goddesses and people are naked or showing their vagina or penis or doing things with their vagina or penis. Never ever have a cover showing someone meditating because everyone knows that meditation was discovered in America. And then exported to the rest of the world. As a global super brand.

Always end your book with Mahatma Gandhi saying something about Hinduism. Then quickly mention something about his sex life and use the words "naked young girls" in the sentence. Because you love Hinduism. And its openness.

Because you care.

2

WHO IS A HINDU?

What does it mean to be a Hindu? Some would say a Hindu is what a Hindu does. And what does a Hindu do? This question is of the greatest importance because for so many Hindus, their faith is about the fulfillment of customs and rituals they have known for generations, hence the constant reference to Hinduism is as a "way of life." I believe that the phrase "way of life" lacks the depth to capture the profundity of Hinduism and is often used so colloquially that it has lost all meaning. But it is undeniable that it captures an everyday essence of doing things—various little acts and rituals that construct meaning for countless believers. There is also a geographical aspect to this. The Persians, who considered the River Sindhu (Indus) as one of the boundaries to their empire, supposedly could not manage the "s" in the river's name and replaced its pronunciation with an "h" to suit their own tongue. Everyone who lived south of the Sindhu (now Indus) came to be called Hindu and this, it is said, is how Hinduism got its name. North of the river was the mountainous terrain that was the land route to Central Asia through Afghanistan. Countless invasions from the Islamic world through the medieval period of Indian history occurred along this path, including one led by Zahir-ud-din Muhammad Babur, from Samarkhand, who had two powerful bloodlines flowing through him—those of Tamerlane and Genghis Khan—Turk and Mongol. Babur founded the Mughal Empire.

But can the birth of our identity as Hindus be that simple? Are linguistics and geography our raison d'être? This query is far from frivolous because it strikes at the heart of a question that has been asked since our independence in 1947—if Pakistan is the land of the Muslims, created specifically as such, then, conversely, is India indisputably the land of the Hindus? The Constitution of India answers "no." It envisions a secular state in which each individual and community finds a place. But, nearly seventy years after independence, this question has become still more urgent to address as it is raised again and again in Indian politics—both internal and external—with regard to the relationship between Hinduism and the State of India, how that relationship has evolved, and where it stands today.

For as long as I can remember, there has been relentless debate in India about whether or not this vast, multicultural, pluralistic nation is, or is not, the land of the Hindus. This debate reverberates not just within a sociopolitical context but also becomes ultimately personal as the idea of a sacred homeland—the abode of its gods and goddesses, and of its consciousness—is so fundamental to Hinduism. The phrase "land of the Hindus" has been used and abused by polemicists of every political allegiance in support of various statements—some that are absolutely ridiculous—that are disrespectful of the enlightened and unique history of India. The question has been furiously debated, often with every side coming to the table with an agenda—and yet, it is important to note that, in the understanding of the common Hindu and in a deliberative analysis of the query, the answer is not thorny or irretrievably complex. The answer lies in the practice of Hinduism and is verified by numerous historical authorities.

With regard to collective identity, then, the question to ask is, what really defines the collective memory of a nation? How does it take shape in national consciousness? What are the characteristics that define its boundaries? Is it not true that a nation is, in reality, first and foremost a subconscious construct? You imagine the nation before it exists, and so it exists. In the colonial narrative, there was no "India" before the British consolidated more parts of the subcontinent under one political rule than had ever existed in the region before. This is, more or less, the central theme of James Mill's three-volume *History of British India*.[1]

Mill—political theorist, historian, and father of John Stuart Mill (who later gave us *On Liberty*[2])—argued, in essence, that India was a regressive dark hole until the light of the English renaissance via colonial rule shone on it. "A duly qualified man can obtain more knowledge of India in one year in his closet in England than he could obtain during the course of the longest life, by the use of his eyes and ears in India,"[3] James Mill wrote, thus presumably eradicating the need to visit a country and meet its people before embarking on a grand project to write its history. The political point here is simple: India itself had been invented, so to speak, by its colonial masters, and therefore, where better to understand India than from the books in England? What could one learn in India? Better to learn from those who invented India—its victorious colonial rulers.

Some of James Mill's harshest words were for Hindus and the Hindu culture, which he described as a despicable hell-hole of oppression and drudgery. He writes, "under the glossing exterior of the Hindu, lies a general disposition to deceit and perfidy . . . in truth, the Hindoo [colonial spelling] like the eunuch, excels in the qualities of a slave . . . dissembling, treacherous, mendacious, to an excess which surpasses even the usual measure of uncultivated society." The Hindu, "Cowardly, unfeeling," wrote Mill, was also "in physical sense, disgustingly unclean in their persons and houses."[4] *History of British India*, one of the most influential colonial books ever written about India, was later described by the American historian Thomas Trautmann as "the single most important source of British Indophobia."[5] That India is a colonial construct, and had no locus standi as a civilization, far less as a member of the body politic of nations before colonial rule, is an old argument. In fact, it *is* a colonial argument. It essentially states, and quite correctly so as far as the geographical boundaries were concerned, that before the British Raj arrived in India there had not been a nation-state as we understand the modern concept. This much is true. But does a lack of physical boundaries of a definitive land imply that there was no sense of a culture, bound by religion—used here in its Latin root word sense *ligare*, "to bind"? Of course not; it had been in existence for centuries. And therein lies the nuance of this rather facile debate—at least I think so—for anyone who spends even a little time tracing the history. The idea of a unified, plural, composite, cultural homeland called Bharat or Bharata has existed perhaps for 3,000 years, though it could well be much older, from around the time that the first foundational text of Vedanta literature, the Rig Veda, was composed, compiled, and memorized. Conceptually, how do we understand this metaphysical "Bharat" and how is it different from modern India? Indeed, is it any different? No, not really. On revisiting the idea of collective memory—which is a construct based on historical writings, oral traditions, and myths—we arrive at the conclusion that the imagination of the landscape is far older than what today's maps suggest. The land called Bharat had been conceptualized in sacred texts and everyday rituals long before cartography drew its lines.

Such a motif has been explored in several critical works by academics interested in the subcontinent's ideological beginnings and subsequent contemporary trajectory. In her masterly treatise, *India: A Sacred Geography*, professor of comparative religion and Indian studies at Harvard, Diana Eck writes, "Bharata is not merely a convenient designation for a conglomerate of cultures, such as Europe has been for so much of its history or such as Indonesia has become in modern times. Nor was Bharata ever the name of a political entity like a nation-state, at least until 1947, when it became the proper name of independent India. And yet it is arresting to consider a sense of unity construed in and through the diverse imagined landscape . . . a sense of connectedness that seems to have flourished for many centuries without the need for overarching political expression or embodiment."[6] Here, Eck explains how Bharata has been a philosophical construct complete with broad definitions of borders that almost entirely replicate the conventionally cartographic span of pre-1947 India.

Reinforcing a similar point of view, the scholar T. N. Madan further writes in "Hinduism: An Introductory Essay,"

> When the ancient Brahmanical text *Vishnu Purana* (3rd century AD) describes the Indians as the children of the land called Bharat, which is then described geographically as the country lying to the north of the ocean and south of the snow-clad mountains, it should be remembered that in the traditional worldview the oceans and the mountains are sacred places with their presiding divinities; indeed they are themselves divinities.[7]

This geographical construct has been defined, to use the words of a favorite tutor of the historian Simon Schama, using "the archive of the feet"[8] emphasized for several millennia in hymns, prayers, myths, legends, and countless journeys undertaken by pilgrims. Schama details the geographical theology of an imagined landscape in his seminal work, *Landscape and Memory*.[9] For instance, there are similarities in approach between the geography—in the mind and on the ground— traversed and established by the Hindu *tirtha* (or pilgrimage map) and the Christian notion of towering trees being contemporaries of Christ. The point here is simply this—the tales of theology may not, sometimes, be as far away from history as we imagine. What, after all, is the battle between Israel and Palestine but the urgent power of theology on geography where the legends of faith have been brought to life and dispute over the land? In 1920, the historian Radhakumud Mookerji spoke about such imagined boundaries of Bharata when he referred to the river hymns of the Vedas. Mookerji writes, "As the mind of the devotee calls up in succession the images of these different rivers defining the limits of his country, it naturally traverses the entire area of his native land and grasps the image of the whole as a visible unit and form." The river hymns of the Rig Veda, said Mookerji, were the "first national conception of Indian unity such as it was."[10] This reference to knowledge of geography also comes, as the historian A. K. Mazumdar has noted, in Alexander Cunningham's *The Ancient Geography of India*.[11] Cunningham, the founder of the Archeological Survey of India, elucidates how the ancient Hindus knew the approximate shape and size of their own land; how the distances to places across the country were known and measured in *krosankas* or milestones. The point here is that there was always a clear understanding of the measure and breadth of the geography that constitutes the nation. At every level, whether through myth or history or popular distance measurement, the geography of the nation was deeply embedded in popular imagination.

Of course, there are more traditional arguments in favor of the idea that nothing called India existed before there was a definitive map. In this line of thinking, until the literal colonial (and then with partition, postcolonial) demarcation of the modern boundaries of India was charted, there was no entity called India. Why does this matter? The point is that if there was no India as such, then how could it have a consistent national civilizational value? But as Eck explains, this approach is a fundamentally flawed way to look at India, because mythology and geography have always shared a very close linkage in the country's culture and history. The epics like the *Ramayana* and *Mahabharata*, for instance, as well as the Puranas, often describe not just incidents, but detailed locations that have actually existed in the landscape. "Not only was the geography of the land expounded most prominently in Hindu mythological texts, but conversely, Hindu mythology in these texts was constantly grounded in the topography of the land of India,"[12] says Eck. She adds, "There is arguably no other major culture that has sustained over so many centuries, and across such diverse regions, a fundamentally locative or place-oriented world view."[13] It is the *char dham* or the four pilgrimage spots, spread across four corners of the imagined landscape, that patterned and created India's Hindu landscape through countless treks by thousands of pilgrims who archived the first indigenous idea of the Indian nationhood through their feet. It is these itineraries of pilgrims that planted the roots of a dream of the homeland. There is a small but important point to note here, which is often overlooked in polemical debate. The largest part of the history of the land we now know as India involves philosophies of what we today call Hinduism. In that sense, those ancient philosophies are the founding blocks of our civilization. Furthermore, that same foundation has allowed the assimilation of many cultures within it and because of this, the political entity, the nation-state called India, is a secular democracy today. These are two independent ideas that do not have to be in opposition to one another. Both can, and have, coexisted for centuries.

This coexistence is not surprising to any practicing Hindu, nor even to those who are nonpracticing since even atheism is a valid theological and philosophical position in the faith. In fact, such theories are not just confined to Hindus, as Eck also points out; it is in this sacred geography that Muslims built scores of shrines dedicated to saints, to an extent that is even incongruous to the Arabic idea of rigid, monotheistic Islam. In a similar manner, Christians, Sikhs, Jains, Buddhists (India being the birthplace of the Buddha, after all), and even Zoroastrians (who found shelter in India when they were being persecuted in Persia) have shared in the Hindu imagination of a sacred geography that defined the foundation of a plural nationhood, allowing the newer faiths to add their own bricks to this palimpsest (as the first prime minister Jawaharlal Nehru called it) and to assimilate over time. Swami Vivekananda himself made this distinction, "In Europe, political ideas form the national unity. In Asia, religious ideals form the national unity. There must be the recognition of one religion throughout the length and breadth of this land. What do I mean by one religion? Not in the sense of one religion as held among the Christians, or the Mohammedans, or the Buddhists. We know that our religion has certain common grounds, common to all sects, however varying their conclusions may be, however different their claims may be,"[14] he said. Vivekananda adds that there are certain commonalities among all and that "this religion of ours admits of a marvelous variation, an infinite liberty to think, and live our own lives."[15]

What Vivekananda describes here is the Hindu plural imagination that has sustained its civilization for 3,000 to 4,000 years, during which periods the Vedic texts were composed—before the arrival of the Islamic age (800 years of Muslim invasions and then Mughal rule) and British colonial rule (less than 200 years). As R. C. Majumdar explained in the introduction to *The History and Culture of the Indian People*,[16] it is pre-Islamic India that laid the philosophical bedrock for the syncretic, composite culture that India has been able to build; therefore to credit this foremost Hindu imagination of a tolerant geography is neither incorrect, nor is it in any manner, shape, or form discriminatory.

Moreover, this is what the Indian archaeologist D. K. Chakrabarti explained in his masterly essay "Cultural Unity of India," where he uses the discovery of objects and the existence of land routes to map out the ancient cultural unity via the geography, as it were, of India. To make his point, Chakrabarti quotes the British geographer H. J. Mackinder writing in 1922: "The one clear unity which India possessed throughout history has been geographical. In no other part of the world, unless perhaps in South America, are the physical features on a grander scale. Yet nowhere else are they more simply combined into a single region."[17]

But in all this discussion, there is an unanswered question. What if the ancient Vedantists, the Aryans themselves, were outsiders? What if, instead of the sages and ascetics of our imagination, there were marauders on horseback that destroyed an earlier civilization—the Indus Valley civilization—and instead brought an influx of their texts, their chants, their prayers? What if these Vedantists, these Aryans, were not "indigenous"?

Whether the Aryans were truly invaders or not is one of the oldest theological, historical, and political debates in India. Why? Because for a long time, the arguments on both sides depended on the "original" geographical location of the Aryans. This is how the logic went—if the Aryans were indigenous people, their philosophies would be the core of Indian civilizational philosophy. If they were invaders—like Babur from Samarkand and then the British, who attacked India and then set up empires after defeating many local kingdoms—then the roots of Indian civilizational history are lost in the mists of time and nothing is quite authentic. Such debate, often raucous, has gone on and on.

Beyond historians and polemicists, how does the ordinary Hindu approach the debate on the origin of the Aryans? Most historians no longer see the Aryans' entry into India as an outright, gory invasion but instead assert something called Aryan Migration Theory (or AMT). This line of thought, which has nearly universally replaced the earlier Aryan Invasion Theory (or AIT), essentially visualizes less of an invasion and more of a steadily assimilating movement, crisscrossing many routes and gene pools.

Now, let us look at some data. In 2011, the *American Journal of Human Genetics* published the findings of a three-year-long research program led by a team of international scientists which proved that Indians have had the same genetic makeup for the last 60,000 years. At the time of publication, senior scientist Gyaneshwar Chaubey said that the entire AIT was based on "low resolution genetic markers. This time we have used autosomes, which means all major 23 chromosomes, for our studies." He stated, "We have proved that people all over India have common genetic traits and origin. All Indians have the same DNA structure. No foreign genes or DNA has entered the Indian mainstream in the last 60,000 years."[18]

Another member of the team, the molecular biologist Lalji Singh, India's foremost geneticist, added: "The Aryan-Dravidian classification was nothing but a misinformation campaign."[19]

Then there's more. A document published in the *American Journal of Human Genetics* in 2006 shows that, as the writer Sanjeev Sanyal says, "India's population mix has been broadly stable for a very long time and . . . there has been no major injection of Central Asian genes for over 10,000 years."[20]

The point here is that, increasingly, scientific research shows that the old Aryan-Dravidian divide, upon which so much political conflict in India has been built, may have been far less definitive than earlier assumed. As D. K. Chakrabarti has rhetorically asked, "If the Harappan religious beliefs should not be viewed through the lens of later-day Hinduism, with which lens should it be viewed?"[21] He explains that the attempt to "relegate Hinduism to the status of just another 'immigrant' religion in the subcontinental context has a long history and different modern manifestations, including the one which denies Hinduism the privilege of being a single religion and ascribes its current status as the majority religion of India to the decision of the British census operators not to classify people according to their *Saivite*, *Vaishnavite* and myriad affiliations." He also notes that "Hindus preferred to call their religion *sanatana dharma*, a term which occurs in a Sanskrit inscription of 6th century AD."[22]

Now, beyond scientific data and archeological arguments, what is an empirical way of tackling this question?

What if we were to embrace both the Indus Valley civilization and the Aryan texts (classifying them as such, for argument's sake) as our collective foundational legacy of engineering and urban planning on one hand and philosophical, ethical heritage on the other? Why is this the wise thing to do, you ask? Simply because both offer undeniable treasures to our historical bedrock, and placing them in some ideological crossfire is almost horrifyingly comic.

So, what does the Indus Valley civilization bring? Its people were responsible for remarkably nuanced city building, broad roads free of encroachments, diligently designed public and private spaces, and sustainable water resources management, including rainwater harvesting and sanitation—something modern India has failed to achieve so that it now faces water wars and news headlines point out that mobile phones are more rampant than toilets in the country. The Indus Valley civilization as a society, French-born Indologist Michel Danino wrote, was "largely free from warfare or man-made destruction [and] devoid, too, of a glorified ruling elite, military structure."[23] Danino has pointed out that some of the renowned Indus Valley seals show kingly figures in *asanas* or postures (specifically the *mulabandhasana*) of yogic contemplation. It shows, Danino has argued, a rare interweave of the spiritual and the worldly.

On the other end of the spectrum, Aryan influences brought into being what are irrefutably our definitive knowledge texts. For thousands of years, these philosophies, whether written or recited, have formed the uniqueness of the Indian mind. As Sanyal says, "The reality of complex back-and-forth linkages make[s] it very difficult to decode history using the linguistic layers. This may explain why traditional timelines based on linguistics were far shorter than those being suggested now by genetics and technology . . . one does not need either conquest or large-scale migration to drive linguistic and cultural exchange."[24]

In our globalized world, for a period of time it was fashionable to claim that the idea of cultural uniqueness was old-fashioned, even bigoted. Thankfully, that age has passed. We have come to value globalization not as an identity-flattening steamroller than makes us all vehicles of the same brand but rather as endless introductions, endless bursts of understanding and insight into how infinitely varied being human really is. This understanding of managing diversity is repeated again and again in Hindu texts. It is the backbone of the Hindu idea of self and how the self interacts with the universe. In a world where migration from the Middle East to Europe and other parts of the world is growing exponentially, there has never been a more appropriate moment to strengthen the idea of unity in diversity. Globalization began with us cheering our commonalities across cultures, but we are progressing on the journey by celebrating our differences. The question of assimilation is growing deeper and more detailed around us. It is no longer enough to get everyone to wear the same clothes, to eat the same food, watch the same movies or ball games; we now understand that external uniformity does not make us one. So, even as the German Constitution is translated into Arabic to assist the hundreds and thousands of new German citizens who are refugees from the Middle East, we now also understand that globalization and our search for oneness needs to go deeper, unpeeling the real layers of prejudices that the likes of McDonald's or Disney cannot hide.

Even Pico Iyer, the ultimate savant regarding travel, preaches the art of being still. There are philosophical and prosaic reasons to seek stillness. It impacts both the selfish and sublime. Recent research at Stanford shows that multitasking—a prized postmillennial skill—is actually damaging our brains and leaving us hopelessly scrambling, because we are no longer able to award proper attention to any singular activity.

Without that attentiveness, our goals are often unmet and our ambitions unfulfilled, which in turn leads to more multitasking, more damage. The search for stillness also comes from an acute sense of losing our "centers," which many of us constantly feel as we try to multitask our way to success. In a world of flexible work routines, we cannot even seem to find real downtime. Why does this stillness evade us? The search for inner peace can only arise from a society that embraces the concept of inner unity.

When we have been everywhere and seen everything—so much easier in the Internet world than ever before—what remains is the uniqueness of our minds. That is the intelligence of our civilization. If there is one central idea of civilizational intellect, it is the understanding that inner oneness among human beings lies at the heart of understanding the intelligence of the universe. There is less fear of the outsider if the comprehension exists that there is no difference between us and *The Other*.

This notion of unity is the greatest lesson from Indian antiquity; it is the sum of the teachings of the Vedas and the Upanishads—the Indian embracing of diversity comes from these Hindu texts which teach the fundamental alikeness of man.

The Vedic period of Indian history gives us its civilizational intelligence. This intelligence is not just about the complex mathematics or the medicinal prowess of ancient Indians. It is not just about the finesse of textiles or the dexterity of handicrafts (which the Roman historian Pliny the Elder once complained were draining the coffers of Rome whose citizens couldn't get enough of cloth as fine as a whiff of smoke from India).

The Hindu idea of unity in all things is the base on which all meditational practice and what we call mindfulness today stands—it teaches the simple lesson that to know the world one must first know oneself fully and uncompromisingly.

The Hindu idea of learning about the universe and the galaxies and all the life they contain is to simultaneously comprehend the life within each human being. There is something incomprehensibly wise and unfathomably vast about this idea, that to know the universe is to look within. The Greek philosopher Socrates is famous for his statement, recorded by his student Plato, "I know that I know nothing." The Hindu way of looking at this is different. I know that I only know myself—says the Hindu yogi—and therefore I know God. To know myself in its entirety is to know God. The idea that divinity is nothing but the highest manifestation of man is a typical Hindu assertion. All four *Mahavakyas* or the Great Sayings of the Upanishads assert this unity.

1. *Prajñānam Brahma*—the supreme consciousness is the Absolute or the divine (Divine intelligence is Brahman) (Consciousness is infinite, the absolute, the highest Truth)
2. *Ayam Aātmā Brahma*—the Self is the Absolute or the divine (The Self is Brahman) (The Self is the infinite)
3. *Tat Tvam Asi*—You are That (Absolute, divine) (That thou art) (Thou art that)
4. *Aham Brahmasmi*—I am the Absolute or the divine (I am Brahman) (I am that infinite)[25]

All this can be quite befuddling, especially when added to the oft-misunderstood Hindu concept of *maya*—the idea that the world as it appears to most human beings is an illusion and there is deeper truth waiting to be discovered.

The Hindu ascetic Ramana Maharshi used to explain that it is not quite true that the ancients taught that the world is unreal. "They only meant that the world is unreal as the *world* but real as the *Self*, the innermost consciousness. If you consider the world outside the self, it is not real."[26] This is one of the most intriguing assertions for a Hindu. How can the world be unreal as the world—which it clearly is—but real as ourselves? Isn't the world the reality we have to deal with everyday? Do we not exit from that reality when we delve deep within ourselves? I have tried to understand this concept in a simple, ordinary way. The universe that we see is really what we are within. The world looks happy when we are joyous—and gloomy when we are melancholy. The inner and outer worlds reflect one another in a circle of action and reaction, where every action or reaction of ours—determined by what we are feeling within—transforms our experience of the outer world. What, then, is the illusion? The illusion is the division in our minds between the inner and the outer world. The illusion prevents us from seeing unity and forces us to perceive a demarcation that does not exist. It is only when this illusion breaks that we are able to be what Gandhi urged us to be—the change we want to see in the world. This idea of the world as an illusion, "maya," and the "truth" as a unified idea both within and without the self is seminal to the way a Hindu looks at the world. After many years of grappling with this concept, I now have a simple, private understanding of it. I realize that the result of my reality depends on my reaction to it. At every step, every day, our reactions to hundreds of situations determine the outcome of that moment, that day, week, and even year. We can even say that our reactions to people, to ideas, to the monsters in our head determine what we call our destiny. In the vein of this argument, I realized that this striving for inner unity, inner stillness, in ourselves and in all things could actually help in tempering our reactions. How angry can I get at you if I think that you are "also me," and that we are the same? In this method of questioning, I have tried to use the window of reaction to understand the deeper philosophy of oneness that the Vedanta preaches. You may well have another dimension or construct through which you might access this interpretation. But in the end, we are bound to reach the same conclusion since the truth is but one.

The fundamental design of the universe remains consistent. If you know the atomic, you know the cosmic. It only depends on the level of complexity. To truly know yourself is to know the universe—this is at once an incredibly empowering and intimidating idea. The Hindu, it seems to me, has only one thing to fall back upon—intelligence, that which is within.

"Indian civilization," wrote Irishwoman Margaret Elizabeth Noble, who later became a Hindu monk and took the name Sister Nivedita under Vivekananda's tutelage, "has educated its children from the beginning to the supreme function of realizing ideas."[27] Unsurprisingly,

then, as Vamsee Juluri, a writer and teacher of media studies, has reminded us, one of Hinduism's oldest and most revered hymns, the
"Gayatri Mantra," sung every morning by thousands for perhaps 3,000
years or more—is a prayer for illumination, for radiance, for knowledge,
for that intelligence which is eternally enlightening. One of the earliest
and most convincing devotional pleas was for intelligence—not material
blessings, not refuge, not solace, not providence, but intelligence. "Hinduism is about intelligence, more than anything else,"[28] writes Juluri.

Imagine that.

3

WHAT MAKES YOU A HINDU?

What makes you a Hindu? Think about this: How do you know that you are Hindu? What do you do every day, or any day for that matter, that conclusively proves that you are Hindu? I spent two extensive parts of my early life pondering this.

The first such period, as mentioned earlier in the book, was during the many years of my life in a Christian missionary school when I was told that I am a sinner. The second was during the two-and-a-half years I spent as a master's student at the AJK Mass Communication Research Centre at Jamia Millia Islamia in New Delhi. These years developed a deep curiosity in me about Christianity and Islam, and the Hindu inter- action and response to them.

During my readings on Christianity and Islam—and their troubled and fascinating journey in India—I have been moved by the profound, therapeutic silence of the cathedral and the poetry of Islamic devotion. I have attended masses and prayer services—and, indeed, I have prayed—in more churches and cathedrals around the world than I can recall. Even today, one of my favorite things to do is to spend time at quaint (and quiet) cathedrals in small European towns. At London's St Martin-in-the-Fields, listening to its famed free afternoon classical mu- sic recitals, I have wondered why more temples don't have Hindustani or Carnatic music concerts. In my solemn moments, the poetry of the Sufi mystics has comforted me.

In the course of time, I spent years having conversations with practicing Muslims and Christians about their faith, people who believed and believed themselves to be believers. Through it all, one distilled thought emerged: more often than not, the practicing Muslim or Christian is more certain about what constitutes an identity of "being Muslim" or "being Christian." The idea of "being Hindu" is far more amorphous, esoteric even. Its spectrum is vast; its canvas touches everything from *Naga sadhus* on river banks to couch potatoes addicted to television serials depicting the imagined shenanigans of gods and goddesses.

But what, if anything, do they have in common? Is there a foundation of belief(s) that define the Hindu? Where is the common ground? I had heard relentless chatter about India's, indeed Hinduism's, diversity, but what about its soul unity? What has kept Hinduism intact for thousands of years as the bearer of a living civilization while all others— Egyptian, Greek, and Roman—have died out? What binds this diversity together? What churns this endless assimilation which, no matter who the conqueror is, keeps its identity animate?

"The chief difference," wrote historian R. C. Majumdar, "between India and the other ancient countries . . . lies in the continuity of her history and civilization. . . . The icons discovered at the Mohenjodaro are those of gods and goddesses who are still worshipped in India, and Hindus . . . repeat even today the Vedic hymns which were uttered on the banks of the Indus nearly four thousand years ago."[1]

As one of India's greatest writers, Bankim Chandra Chatterjee, wrote, "With other peoples, religion is only a part of life; there are things religious and there are things lay and secular. . . . To the Hindu his relations with God and man, his spiritual and temporal life are incapable of being distinguished. They form one compact and harmonious whole, to separate which into components is to break the entire fabric."[2]

But why does this continuity exist? What is this knowledge that binds Hindus over thousands of years? What relevance could it possibly retain from century to century?

In my small journey through the faith, I have found that the answer is that Hinduism survives because it sets people free. What does that mean? Let us consider the absolute basic meaning. The fundamental difference between Islam and Christianity, and Hinduism, is their differing approaches to understanding and explaining the nature of truth.

All religions are concerned with truth or the purpose of human existence. What does human life mean? What does it achieve? What is it all for? Where does it all lead? And how can we make it better? Aren't these in essence the questions that every religion or faith explores?

The answer, according to Islam and Christianity, is to become better. How does one become better? By following a revelation that comes from the one to which it was revealed. And where is it contained, this revelation, its lessons, its exhortations? It is contained in words in a book.

In Hinduism, there is no truth to be found outside oneself.

"All this universe is Brahman. The self of all beings is Brahman,"[3] says the *Mandukya Upanishad*. "He who sees the self in all beings and all beings in the self, henceforth, has no more remorse," says the *Isha Upanishad*. The truth is hidden behind maya, "the cosmic ignorance thrown up by the material world."[4]

"The recognition that the world and its contents are an illusion, that material objects inevitably decay, that skills and talents fade, that no relationship lasts forever, is the first step towards *moksha* or enlightenment,"[5] the philosopher Kenan Malik has explained.

The first step to knowing the truth is to acknowledge that it does not lie outside since everything outside is an illusion. But that's just step one. The next, more vital step is to comprehend what is within. "One only comes to know the self, the Upanishads suggest, by becoming the self, and one only becomes the self by recognizing that at some fundamental level the self and the world are one,"[6] writes Malik.

In the epilogue of the book that made him famous (*What Is Life?*), German Nobel Prize–winning nuclear physicist Erwin Schrödinger explained, "Consciousness is never experienced in the plural, only in the singular. . . . Consciousness is a singular of which the plural is un-known."[7]

Schrödinger is best known today for his thought experiment famous-ly known as "Schrödinger's Cat." What happens in this experiment is that a cat is left in a chamber with a flask of poison containing a radioac-tive element. As the element decays, the flask breaks and the cat dies, but how does one know whether the cat is dead or alive until it is observed? Until the time it is observed, the cat can be said to be both dead and alive. The most common interpretation of this experiment is that any system stops being a superposition of states (the cat is both dead and alive) and becomes one or the other once an observation happens. It is the act of observation that defines the final state, and the two are irretrievably connected.

Quantum physics breaks away from the thinking that, at the funda-mental level, the reality of the universe is what American theoretical physicist David Bohm calls "elementary parts" which constitute every-thing (in various complexities), and that these elementary parts can be separately analyzed.

Instead, quantum physics shows that reality at the very fundamental level is an unbroken wholeness, an essential interconnectedness where the object being analyzed changes with the situation of the observer, and it is this interconnected reality that is the most fundamental truth. That's why Schrödinger wrote that what seems to us as plurality is "merely a series of different aspects" of the same thing, the same truth. "Sensory deception" or what the Hindus call *maya* gives us an illusion of many-ness where the reality is but one.

Schrödinger understood the commonality between the scientific theories he was working on and the metaphysical knowledge of the Vedanta. He wrote, "This life of yours which you are living is not merely a piece of this entire existence, but in a certain sense the whole; only this whole is not so constituted that it can be surveyed in one single glance. This, as we know, is what the Brahmins express in that sacred mystic formula which is yet really so simple and so clear: *tat tvam asi*, this is you. Or, again, in such words as—I am in the east and the west, I am above and below, I am in this entire world."[8]

This was not just esoteric mystical rambling. Walter Moore, biographer of Erwin Schrödinger, wrote that the scientist saw that the concepts of unity detailed in the Vedanta resonate with the "unity and continuity of wave mechanics."[9] It was men of science—and not sages or ascetics—like Schrödinger and German theoretical physicist Werner Heisenberg who altered the vision and understanding of modern physics from "a model of a great machine composed of separable interacting material particles" to "a universe based on superimposed inseparable waves of probability amplitudes." It is a view that any student of the Vedanta would immediately recognize as apt, *tat*, naturally knows the Vedanta, must finally lead to *asi*.

John Wheeler, the theoretical physicist who coined the term "black hole," detailed this even further. He said in essence that quantum mechanics dissolved the old scientific term of the "observer" and brought in a new term that the Eastern mystics always knew to be true, that of the "participator." "Nothing is more important about the quantum principle than this, that it destroys the concept of the world as 'sitting out there,' with the observer safely separated. Even to observe so minuscule an object as an electron, he must reach in. He must install his chosen measuring equipment. It is up to him to decide whether he shall measure position or momentum. Moreover, the measurement changes the state of the electron. The universe will never afterwards be the same. In some strange sense the universe (therefore) is a participatory universe."[10]

The *Atman*, the soul, or the essence of the soul, the self, as it were, fuses into the *Brahman*, or the essence of the universe—and to understand that is to attain enlightenment.

"The manifestation of Brahman in the human soul is called Atman,"[11] wrote Fritjof Capra in his best-selling book, *The Tao of Physics*. He explains why Eastern faiths and their philosophies are closest to science, and distills this idea which he calls the "unity of all things." "The most important characteristic of the Eastern worldview—one could almost say the essence of it—is the awareness of the unity and mutual interrelation of all things and events, the experience of all phenomena in the world as manifestations of a basic oneness,"[12] Capra wrote. "All things are seen as interdependent and inseparable parts of this cosmic whole; as different manifestations of the same ultimate reality."[13] Or as the *Mundaka Upanishad* says, "*Brahmaivedam-amrtam*" (This whole manifested universe is the immortal Brahman.)[14] Capra's point is that what ancient Hindu texts express as a mystical experience is quite close to what modern atomic physics describes as an interconnected cosmic phenomenon.

As Werner Heisenberg, one of the pioneers of quantum mechanics, discoverer of the Heisenberg uncertainty principle and winner of the Nobel Prize in Physics in 1932, said, "Natural science does not simply describe and explain nature; it is part of the interplay between nature and ourselves."[15]

So far so confusing.

Does this mean—literally—that people in India knew thousands of years ago what quantum physics has, and is, discovering in the modern age? Frankly, most rational people would dismiss such a grandiose, sweeping statement. If we were to accept such a broad statement then it would lead to all sorts of nativistic aggrandizements. There is a better way of explaining this.

To understand how, I spoke to Ankur Barua who teaches Hindu studies at the University of Cambridge. He first studied physics at the graduate level, then switched to read theology, and now lectures at the Faculty of Divinity, Cambridge.

First of all, when it is said that some theories of quantum theories are similar to "Hinduism," what Hinduism are we really talking about?

We are talking about the Upanishads written in a period starting from about 800 years to 500 years before the birth of Christ. The accumulated knowledge of the Upanishads is what we refer to as the Vedanta.

To understand this, Barua explained, you need to understand two terms—*idealism* and *realism*. In philosophical parlance, realism is the belief that the existence of everyday material objects around you is in no way dependent on you perceiving them.[16] This means, for instance, a box of food that you put in your refrigerator exists there even when you are not looking at it. This is almost common sense. Idealism is the view that the existence of so-called material objects is somehow dependent on you perceiving them.

When we talk about the correspondence between quantum mechanics and Upanishadic knowledge, we are really talking in terms of an idealistic interpretation or understanding of quantum physics and of the Upanishads. Physicists and philosophers who argue in favor of this view opine that if the idealistic interpretations of both systems are compared, since they are both idealistic, they must therefore correspond.

Why would anyone want to be an idealist? Take a bottle. What is a bottle really? It is a bundle of sensations, isn't it? Some are visual, some tactile, some olfactory, etc., right? A combination of five senses is involved in perceiving the bottle. Now think about this. These five categories of sensations, what are they? They are mental events. And mental events are just ideas. So this is an idea, this bottle is an idea. Why do you want to go beyond these ideas? It is much more economical to just say that all I mean by a bottle—or matter—is an aggregate of mental sensations, of ideas. So what have I done? I have demonstrated the dependence on the mind of so-called matter or matter's dependence on the mind. So we are inching towards an idealist view.

Classical physics is almost always unreflexively realist. In classical physics, for example, I can tell through some calculations the precise location of the moons of Jupiter. I don't have to look at them. The fact that I am not looking at them does not alter their physical location or momentum in any way. When we move into the subatomic domain (the domain of quantum physics), subatomic phenomena are extremely queer and mysterious and complex and mind-boggling and counterintuitive. Somehow we are not able to determine with completely certainty and exactitude both the position and the momentum of one of these subatomic particles. So if you observe them, somehow their positions seem to change.

Since 1925 (the birth of quantum physics) there has been a huge argument on this—if quantum mechanics is our most established science and everything works according to it, what is the best metaphysical explanation for it?

Broadly, Barua explained to me, we need to understand two ways of looking at this. One is called *Instrumentalism*. This says actually there is nothing very deep happening in quantum physics. It is just a set of equations correlating theories with predictions. It does not give you any inkling on the deep knowledge of reality.

The other is called the *Idealistic Interpretation* of quantum mechanics. Some physicists like Henry Stapp (Berkeley) have worked on this. And it is their work that recognizes the role of perception in the manifestation of phenomena which corresponds to some ideas of the Upanishads.

Now it is important to note that there is no "realism" or "idealism" in the Upanishads. Such concepts are of a much later date. Adi Shankaracharya, the Indian monk (788–820 CE) who propounded the *Advaita Vedanta* philosophy—to which quantum mechanics is most commonly compared—is not interested in materialism or science; his goal is the spiritual. His goal is much further—it is the Brahman. Brahman, loosely, can be translated as God. *Advaita Vedanta* in essence provides a cohesive interpretation to the entire Upanishadic knowledge and argues that all that we see or experience is merely a manifestation of the Brahman or God. It says that in essence we, ourselves, are God, as in everything we perceive is nothing but the Brahman. As the nineteenth-century monk Vivekananda, a major modern proponent of *Advaita Vedanta*, explained: "Each soul is potentially divine." We are all God or we all have God within us—we just haven't realized it yet.

Now to come to the question of correspondence with quantum mechanics—is there a world independent from human cognition? Shankaracharya says no. The so-called material world is a transformation, a manifestation of the Brahman. If you told Shankara about the idealistic interpretation of quantum mechanics, he would say—well, that's only a halfway house. You have only gone halfway. Sure, all of this is maya (illusion), etc.—but what about the Brahman? Where is the eternal, timeless, indivisible Brahman?

So the point is—it is an upside-down positioning to say oh, the sages of the Upanishads "knew quantum physics." In a sense, that is not just incorrect, it is also underselling the Upanishads. The way to put it is—if Adi Shankara were to come alive today, he would recognize or understand many theories of quantum physics easily. Or today, after we have read and understood quantum physics, when we go back and read the Upanishads, we recognize many echoes or threads in it from the theories of quantum physics.

Ankur Barua said that this has brought him to a position he calls "religious agnosticism," that is, there are no good logical arguments that conclusively either establish or negate the possibility of something beyond time and space. One would like to believe that the universe is hospitable to human flourishing—that somehow the universe is not running against those values (kindness, for instance) that we human beings hold to be important. But one can't demonstrate it inexorably.

This is explained in a different but equally powerful way in the introduction to Ken Wilber's *Quantum Questions: Mystical Writings of the World's Greatest Philosophers*. Wilber, an American writer on mysticism, philosophy, and science, collected together in this book thoughts on mysticism from some of the greatest scientists the world has ever known—physicists Werner Heisenberg, Erwin Schrödinger, Albert Einstein, Louis de Broglie, James Jeans, Max Planck, Wolfgang Pauli, and Arthur Eddington. Wilber asks a basic question in the book, how is it that all these physicists, some of the finest minds on the subject, "rejected the notion that physics proves or even supports mysticism, and yet every one of them was an avowed mystic"?[17]

Does that mean that modern physics can easily dismiss what Wilber calls "mysticism" (so much of Hinduism's core ideas can be placed in the realm of mysticism)? On the contrary, Wilber explains that these great physicists were steeped in mysticism because they realized that modern physics was grasping bits and pieces of the reality that mysticism interprets. Wilber quotes Eddington as saying that "the frank realization that physical science is concerned with a world of shadows is one of the most significant of recent advances."[18]

The point here is that physics—scientists today understand—grasps only an image, a shadow, a mathematical picture of reality, and not reality itself. James Jeans writes: "Many would hold that, from the broad philosophical standpoint, the outstanding achievement of twentieth-century physics is not the theory of relativity with its welding together of space and time, or the theory of quanta with its present apparent negation of the laws of causation, or the dissection of the atom with the resultant discovery that things are not what they seem: it is the general recognition that we are not yet in contact with ultimate reality."[19]

Eddington adds: "Physics most strongly insists that its methods do not penetrate behind the symbolism."[20] Echoing Jeans, "We are still imprisoned in our cave, with our backs to the light, and can only watch the shadows on the wall."[21]

This is the common ground between the mysticism of Hinduism and modern science. Modern science recognizes that it sees only a part of the Truth. Hindu mysticism realizes, too, that science is, as it were, a partial verification of the ultimate Truth. As Barua told me, it would be incorrect to say the ancient sages knew "quantum physics." But there are echoes. Once you understand modern physics and then you go back and read the ancient Hindu texts—you hear distinct echoes. As my friend, the cosmology enthusiast Ishira Mehta, is fond of saying, "It is almost that modern science is verifying, accurately, logically, some things which the ancient mystics knew in somewhat of an instinctive manner." Eddington understood this when he wrote: "Surely then that mental and spiritual nature of ourselves, known in our minds by an intimate contact transcending the methods of physics, supplies just that . . . which science is admittedly unable to give."[22] The renowned string theorist Edward Witten has admitted the limitations of science to decipher consciousness in a recent interview with the following words:

> I think consciousness will remain a mystery. Yes, that's what I tend to believe. I tend to think that the workings of the conscious brain will be elucidated to a large extent. Biologists and perhaps physicists will

understand much better how the brain works. But why something that we call consciousness goes with those workings, I think that will remain mysterious. I have a much easier time imagining how we understand the Big Bang than I have imagining how we can understand consciousness.[23]

This comprehension of consciousness is, to me, the greatest legacy of the Hindu mind.

What does all this mean to me as a practicing Hindu? It means I feel—and have felt consistently—at once unbelievably free and surreally bewildered. As you peel off layers of rituals that exemplify everyday Hindu practice, you realize—at least I have—that none of it is designed as a final, unalterable route. It is all a morphing, changing, experiential process wherein the final destination is the same not just for me but for every single living being (since the essence of all life is the same), *but* the journey can vary infinitely.

"The truth for the Hindu," wrote Michel Danino, "is inexhaustible; there can be no end to the revelation, no only child, no last prophet. No Indian teacher ever said that his message was final and there could be nothing beyond it. Anyone is free to start a new teaching, give a new message to the world, found a new school of thought."[24]

Why does such liberty exist? Because Hinduism teaches that no matter what the path or methodology, finally all seekers of the truth will arrive at the same destination. That's why Hindus find it easy to accept other faiths as entirely valid; after all, whether it is Christ, Moses, or Muhammad, the destination is the same, says Hinduism.

There is a lovely little story I was told as a child by my parents about the spiritual teacher Ramakrishna Paramhansa who was asked how he could justify the worship of clay idols; surely God is formless?

"You believe God is without form; that is quite all right. But never for a moment think that this alone is true and all else false. Remember that god with form is just as true as God without form. But hold fast to your own conviction,"[25] said Paramhansa.

The questioner was adamant. "But," he said, "one should explain to those who worship the clay image that it is not God, and that while worshipping it, they should have God in view and not the clay image. One should not worship clay."[26]

Paramhansa answered, "This is the one hobby of you Calcutta people—giving lectures and bringing others to the light! Nobody ever stops to consider how to get the light himself. Who are you to teach others? God has arranged all these forms to suit different people in different stages of knowledge." The idols that my school preachers paid so much attention to were merely incidental in the path to discovering pure consciousness.

In this journey, Paramhansa is saying what pioneering psychiatrist Carl Jung, who was immensely influenced by the Ramakrishna Mission and Paramhansa's teachings, said, "the individual will never find the real justification for his existence, and his own spiritual and moral autonomy anywhere except in an extramundane principle capable of relativizing the overpowering influence of external factors. The individual who is not anchored in God can offer no resistance on his own resources to the physical and moral blandishments of the world."[27]

At this point, it is easy to think that Jung is wrong. Surely in a world that has always fought over whose God is better, and still does, requires not more religion, but less? But that's exactly the point. Jung's understanding of God realization is noncompetitive, non-exclusivist, and non-threatening. It seeks no convert or kingdom. It is an entirely internal journey of self-discovery. Jung wrote, "he [the human being] needs the evidence of inner, transcendent experience which alone can protect him from the otherwise inevitable subversion in the mass."[28]

It is to keep the sanctity of this sacred internal journey that Jung spoke against the dictator state when he argued, "along with the individual it swallows up his religious forces. The State has taken the place of God; that is why, seen from this angle, the socialist dictatorships are religious and State slavery is a form of worship. But the religious function cannot be dislocated and falsified in this way without giving rise to secret doubts, which are immediately repressed so as to avoid conflict with the prevailing trends towards mass-mindedness. The result, as always in such cases, is overcompensation in the form of *fanaticism*, which in its turn is used as a weapon for stamping out the least flicker of opposition."[29]

Jung makes for critical reading to understand the difference between an internal and external spiritual journey. He is as vehemently against the rule of the dictatorial state (in his time especially concerned with the excesses of the eastern European Communist countries) as he as against dogmatic religion. His focus, as the Eastern religions have always held to be true, is man's search for the truth within. Eastern philosophies, said Jung, shifted the "centre of gravity from the ego to the self, from man to god."[30]

In Roberto Calasso's *Ardor*, which is the retelling of the wisdom of the Vedic age, there is this utterly enlightening conversation between Yajnavalkya—the pupil of Surya (the sun god) and the master of all *yajnas* or sacrifices—and the sublimely wise King Janak. Janak asks Yajnavalkya, "What happens after death?"

Yajnavalkya talks neither of heaven nor hell or everlasting life, nor sin or salvation. He says what happens after death is that we become "that person which is reflected of us in the eye of another person looking at us."[31]

Just think about the deceptively simple but overwhelming worth of that answer. We become the image in the eye of another. Why? Because we are not the senses. We are that which observes the senses and the ego.

If you think about this, you will realize that this is exactly what the Adi Shankaracharya is famously singing about in his most glorious hymn

Chidananda rūpah Shivoham Shivoham
manobuddhyahaṃ
kāra cittāni nāhaṃ
na ca śrotrajihve na ca ghrāṇanetre na ca vyoma bhūmir na tejo na vāyuḥ
cidānandarūpa śivo'ham śivo'ham[32]

It translates as: I am not mind, nor intellect, nor ego, nor the reflections of inner self (*citta*). I am not the five senses. I am beyond that. I am not the ether, nor the earth, nor the fire, nor the wind (the five elements). I am indeed, that eternal knowing and bliss, the auspicious (*Śivam*), love and pure consciousness.

Or, as Vivekananda said, "Never forget the glory of human nature! We are the greatest god. . . . Christs and Buddhas are but waves on the boundless ocean which I am."[33] The "I" here is not Vivekananda but the common pure consciousness in every human. The notion that the human being could find within himself the source of the divine and is, therefore, everywhere and in everything—since the divine is everywhere—is the glue that holds together the Hindu worldview; it is both the cornerstone and the wings of the faith.

This idea is often almost unfathomable. That which is in us—the pure consciousness that observes all our senses, emotions, and ego and is beyond it all—is what we really are. And that pure consciousness is common to every living thing on earth. It is an idea that inevitably stops you in your tracks. It is an idea to end all ideas: in essence, every living thing is the same.

In a video that has gone viral, astrophysicist Neil deGrasse Tyson, the Fredrick P. Rose Director of the Hayden Planetarium at the Rose Centre for Earth and Space in New York, has explained it as "the most astounding fact" about the universe.

> Many people feel small, because they're small and the universe is big, but I feel big, because my atoms came from those stars. There is a level of connectivity. That's really what you want in life, you want to feel connected, you want to feel relevant. You want to feel like you're a participant in the goings on of activities and events around you. That's precisely what we are, just by being alive.[34]

Just by being alive, at every single moment, you are not just part of the universe, you are the universe.

In the Upanishads, there are two marvelous little set pieces that illuminate this idea. Both are very short conversations between a man and a son.

In the first, the father asks the son to fetch him the fruit of a banyan tree. It goes like this:

Father: Fetch me a fruit.

Son: Here it is, Father.

Father: Break it open.

Son: I have broken it. Here.

Father: What do you see?

Son: Very tiny seeds, Father.

Father: Break one seed.

Son: Here it is; I have broken it.

Father: Now what do you see?

Son: Nothing.

Father: What you cannot see, my son, is the essence, and in that essence this giant banyan tree lives. In that essence is the Self of all that is. That is the truth; that is the Self. And you are that Self too.

In the other story, the father asks the son to put some salt in a glass of water at night and bring it to him in the morning. In the morning, when the son does that, the father asks him to remove the salt from the water and bring it to him. But the son cannot do that because the salt has dissolved. The following conversation ensues:

Father: Now taste the water from the top. How does it taste?

Son: Salty.

Father: Taste the water from the middle of the glass.

Son: This tastes salty too.

Father: Finally, taste the water from the bottom. How about that? How does it taste?

Son: This also tastes of salt.

Father: You don't understand the one reality that is in your body, my son, but it is there. Everything is that one reality, that one essence. Everything is that soul. And you are nothing but that reality, that soul.

But what does all of this really mean in your life and mine? To me, at least, this idea has been infinitely liberating. Here's why: For a moment, think of the object that is most precious to you. Maybe it is a ball or an old gramophone, a pen, a clock, a wicker basket, or a skipping rope. All of these objects, indeed any of them, can be worshipped by you as God. For any object can be, as long as the belief is strong and resilient, equally valid as a representative form of the divine. There is absolutely nothing that, if held in great affection and reverence, cannot be considered as a form of the Almighty to be worshipped.

There is no form, no shape, no size, and no color that is considered unworthy as long as it is revered by the worshipper. Notice how the main thing here is not what the representative item is but the reverence of the worshipper. It is the reverence—indeed the meditative reverie— of the believer that constitutes the sanctity of the sacred, not the object per se. As Alan Watts wrote, "If you ask me to show god, I will point to the sun, or a tree, or a worm. But if you say 'You mean, then, god is the sun, the tree, the worm, and all other things?' I shall have to say that you have missed the point entirely."[35]

When I was a child in Calcutta, the festival of Durga Puja came upon us with the weather. The searing heat of Calcutta, languorous and all abuzz in flames at the same time, dissipated to a carefree autumn during this time. Durga Puja was my favorite festival. The celebrations continued—and they do today—for ten long days. The air is fresh and fragrant and the mood exuberant. Durga Puja celebrates the victory of good over evil but it is actually more complicated than that. It holds within it an emblem of the power of Indian feminist thought—the goddess destroying the arrogance of an all-powerful man, a man so intellectually strong and devoted that he has been blessed by the gods. The man in question, *Mahishasura*, prays ardently to the gods for a very long time and wins the right to ask for a boon. What does he ask for? He asks for immortality. But that is one thing that the gods cannot give— for to be immortal is to be a god. It is not possible for man to get that virtue. So instead, *Mahishasura* wins the boon that he cannot be killed by any *man*. The all-powerful warrior does not believe that any woman can kill him. Once he wins the boon, he is able to defeat all the gods who then pool together their powers into the form of a goddess who battles Mahishasura. When I was a child, we were taught how the warrior is defeated by the goddess and killed not because he is not a great warrior or because he is evil. He isn't. But above all his wonderful qualities, he has one critical flaw. He is arrogant. Given the powers of near immortality, he is unable to use them for good.

My mother used to take the opportunity of Durga Puja to drill into my head that I should not be "overconfident." Overconfidence was a great sin in our little world. We were taught to be cautious—diligent but not too brazen. There was philosophy in this teaching. My parents believed, as they often said, in the philosophical lesson of the Vedan-ta—that one must act in the righteous way without expecting reward. And even though their lives had very few material comforts, it is a concept that they held dear. It was curious for me to see this while growing up because the festival of Durga Puja was so irretrievably tied to the material aspects of life—the purchase of new clothes, the eating of vast feasts, the endless partying, the massive *pandals* made of wood and heavily decorated to hold the giant idols of the goddess during the days of the *Puja*. Yet, we were taught to see through all that and focus on the subliminal message—do not be greedy, do not be arrogant. This focus on the cerebral over the material gave us the aesthetic and ethical mooring to enjoy a festival of excess. There was a sense, I always felt, of looking beyond the obvious and trying to understand the ideas that lay behind the immediate raucousness. Even as we shopped and ate and drank, the prayers every morning were solemn, and often required the discipline of a short morning fast before the ceremony—one was allowed to eat only after the prayers were over. It helped that the priests who conducted the ceremonies were often from villages near Calcutta and mostly men of extremely modest financial means. They added the grace of austerity to the ceremonies.

During Durga Puja, one of the seminal ceremonies is the *pran pratishtha*, the prayer to put life in the idol of the mother goddess. As a child, I found it fascinating to watch the priest lovingly pray to bring the goddess to life with mantras and the final touch, the painting of the eyes. It took me years, in fact decades, to truly appreciate what I was seeing.

Step back and think. In this one act of pran pratishtha, man imbibes the divinity within to bring God to life. What could be a more powerful and potent symbol of the unified inner divinity of the universe? Man at his worshipful best reaches a point in prayer wherein he or she is able to invest in the idol the divinity of life. And man is able to do this because there is no difference in the pure consciousness between man and God; both man and God are manifestations of basic oneness.

That's why Hinduism has *devas* and *asuras*—manifestations of devotion, mischief, good, and evil. Man, says Hinduism, has the potential to go higher or lower in this chain of divinity. Man can make the journey from *nar* (human) to *narayan* (a god-like manifestation), or could turn to baser instincts. Even asuras (demigods) are not "evil" per se but merely less evolved manifestations of divinity. For instance, *Ravan* is not just a "demon" as many Western writers put it, but a scholar of the Vedic texts, enormously learned and capable of astonishing feats of worship and penance. It is Ravan who has the capability, in the legend, to build a stairway to heaven, but distracted by his whims and baser instincts, he fails to complete it. That's why avatars are but manifestations, divinity in different forms. We are all manifestations of the same divinity, says Hinduism, but avatars are the highest and most evolved form of that manifestation.

In one sense, Christianity and Hinduism believe in the same thing—
that there are men and women who define the spiritual destiny of
mankind and bring forth a new age of man's deeper engagement with
divinity, both within and without. Both faiths believe in divine incarnation. The difference between the two is this: Christianity believes that
that there is only one true incarnation, "the only begotten son of God"
and does not accept any other incarnations within Christian history or
outside.

Hinduism or sanatana dharma accepts both Christ and the Buddha
as divine incarnations. As Krishna says in the *Bhagavad Gita*, "*sambha-
vami yuge yuge*" (I incarnate age after age). Why, asks the Hindu, can't
God incarnate more than once? In fact, there is no Hindu quarrel even
with prophets like Moses and Muhammad, who are next to incarnates
in divinity. All of these forms are accepted as part of mankind's search
for the eternal truth. There is no conflict with many forms because the
core Vedanta teaching is that the soul was never born and never dies. It
is only the body that changes, is born, and dies. Vivekananda described
it is as a book being turned over. It is the book that turns, he said, not
the man turning it.

In the great Indian epic, the *Mahabharata*, the warrior Arjun, said to
be the greatest archer of all times, dithers on arriving at the battlefield.
He laments, Why should I fight my own cousins? Why should I kill my
own family? It is then that the god Krishna explains to him the concept
of dharma (the closest, though inadequate, translation is duty). It is his
duty as a warrior, Krishna tells Arjun, to defend what is good and fight
what is wrong. This dialogue is known as the *Bhagavad Gita*. It is
equally a philosophical treatise as a spiritual one. In this Krishna also
tells Arjun, "*Mahatmanastu mam Partha daivin prakrtimasritah; Bha-
jantyananya manaso jnatva bhutadimavyayam.*"[36] It translates as: The
mahatmas or the noble ones, Partha (the other name of Arjun),
endowed with divine qualities, worship me with single-minded devotion, for they know me as the imperishable source of all beings.

The idea that man can invoke divinity in clay to make it God and
then worship it is, to me, the most sublime idea of the potential in each

of us; the idea that not one of us is condemned. Not one of us needs saving or an external aid. All that we seek, all that we will ever need and could ever need, lies within us.

The Hindu believes that no one is a heathen. No one is an infidel. Not one of us is an unbeliever, for how can you be an unbeliever in yourself? There are no false gods because how can that which lies within you, which you worship, be false to you? How can you be false to yourself?

You and I, we are manifestations of God. We are God; we just don't know it yet. That is why the sages said, *"Tum jano ya na jano, mano ya na mano, tum hi Ram."* This means: Whether you know it or not, whether you realize it or not, whether you accept it or not, you are the divine.

You and I, we are not sinners. We are the divine. We just don't know it yet.

4

WHO IS THE ONE TRUE GOD?

For a moment think about this. In the history of theology, one question reigns supreme amid the bloodshed—which is the one true God?

Empires rose and fell to defend the one true God, to spread his word (you will notice that "one true God" is usually male) or to destroy the realms of the infidel or the unbeliever and cleanse places, kingdoms, and nations for the rule and supremacy of the only messiah. Even today, thousands of years after the death of the last major messiahs, the bloodshed to establish the reign of the true God continues.

But what if the Hindu point of view was better understood in our world? What if the fundamental premise of Vedanta philosophy seeped into our ethics? What if the very heart of the Hindu argument was better understood?

And what is that core?

Hindus fundamentally believe that there is no one true God. There is, therefore, no false God. Naturally, if you don't have one true God, it is tough to have a false God. And if you don't have one true God or a false God, then there are no unbelievers. For an unbeliever to exist, there must be a static, defined idea of what the manifestation of the Almighty looks like. In its absence, it is very difficult to point fingers at the heretic. Without the finality of the messenger of God—and his words being the final message—how can there be an unchanging idea of the infidel?

Those then are the main questions Hinduism answers with certitude. It says that every manifestation (indeed messenger) of the Almighty has equal validity to propagate its version of the divine truth. In a sense, the Hinduism argument is the opposite of the monotheistic faiths. It says every messenger (or prophet) is to be held true until proved false.

The Hindu path, as Vivekananda famously declared, has no sinners. In this, it takes a position diametrically opposite, for instance, to Christianity. In Hinduism, there are no souls to save and man is born without original sin.

This is why Vivekananda declared at the World's Parliament of Religions in 1893, "The Christian is not to become a Hindu or a Buddhist, nor a Hindu or a Buddhist to become a Christian. But each must assimilate the spirit of the others and yet preserve his individuality and grow according to his own law of growth. . . . The Parliament of Religions . . . has proved . . . that holiness, purity and charity are not the exclusive possessions of any church in the world."

In fact, Hinduism argues for the other extreme. It says, to quote Vivekananda again, "each soul is potentially divine."[1] We must now ask what it means and how my life (or yours) changes with the knowledge that each soul is potentially divine.

I can only explain how I have understood it and how it has worked for me. Once you start to think about this idea that each and every soul—yours included—is potentially divine, you start to get a little nervous. Why? Because it takes away our emotional and psychological crutches. When you realize that, in reality, you have nothing to fall back upon but yourself, it breaches the most secure barriers and fortresses in the mind, those we usually keep protected by the idea of God.

I look at the sonorous statement that each soul is potentially divine as being a bit like the swimming teacher who pushes a trusting child into the deep end just at the moment when the pupil is trying hardest to clutch on to the teacher to avoid swimming alone. The teacher knows that there will be flailing of arms and much water swallowed, but finally the student will learn how to swim. The teacher is there to ensure that his ward does not drown, but beyond that the student is on his own.

In her now famous TED Talk, researcher Brené Brown explains how the word courage comes from the Latin word *cor*, which means heart. It derives from the ability and psychological ability to open your heart and be vulnerable. The root of Hindu philosophy is, to me, like that. It forces you to be on your own, and it pushes you down a personal path explaining that while the truth is one, every journey to reach it must be unique. The path to discover divinity inside you is a path of extreme vulnerability. It is a path fraught with accepting your deepest insecurities and facing your most frightening demons. You cannot, naturally, hope to discover your inherent divine nature until you face your most challenging anxieties.

What happens when you start to realize that behind all that you see as separate aspects of life or manifestations—other people, animals, plants, and everything living—there is in reality one, unbroken, uniform oneness of consciousness?

Perhaps it might be useful here, just for simplification, to use the word "soul" instead of pure consciousness or consciousness. What if you were to begin to see everyone around you not as who they appear to be—not their body type, nationality, skin color, speech distinctions, and character distinctions—but just simply as other souls exactly like yours, for these are part of the universal soul?

Think about what that does to our numerous constructs of division on the basis of color, class, wealth, education, and even physical abilities. It is, I think, impossible to instantaneously comprehend the importance of this. This understanding of a fundamental commonness that goes indefinitely beyond political correctness or ideology opens the canvas of our mind infinitely and allows us to recreate an identity step by step with increasing awareness.

What this does or has the potential to do to centuries of historical strife is almost incomprehensible. Where would crusades be, for instance, if everyone accepted that there was no one true God? How many millions could and would be saved if the concept of the infidel

were wiped out? What if we were all to agree that there are no unbelievers? Would that not be the single greatest act of conflict resolution
in the history of the world?

Here in my mind is the unique position of the Hindu argument: a
Hindu does not recognize the concept of infidels or unbelievers for he
or she does not believe that there is only one path, one messenger, or
one book to God.

At this point, let us make a further distinction as explained by the
Hindu thinker Rajiv Malhotra. He makes the distinction between tolerance and mutual respect, arguing, "It is fashionable in interfaith discussions to advocate 'tolerance' for other faiths. But we would find it pa-
tronizing, even downright insulting, to be 'tolerated' at someone's dinner table. No spouse would appreciate being told that his or her presence at home was being 'tolerated.' No self-respecting worker accepts
mere tolerance from colleagues. We tolerate those we consider inferior.
In religious circles, tolerance, at best, is what the pious extend towards
people they regard as heathens, idol worshippers or infidels. It is time
we did away with tolerance and replaced it with 'mutual respect.'"[2]

Hinduism argues for a world of mutual respect, where none would
think their path is greater than any other. What this also means is that
Hindus realize (or at least ought to) that for true peace to be achieved,
this mutual respect must be the starting point. Mere tolerance is only a
Band-Aid, a temporary truce that breaks often and violently. A Hindu
recognizes that the tolerance allows the sotto voce demonization of "the
other." To tolerate is to, at best, adjust but rarely ever to integrate. The
Hindu approach is different and aimed at supreme integration.

What if you realized, almost like in a science fiction movie, that it is
the same life force that seamlessly leaves one body and takes the form
of another, and the sum total of that one universal life force never alters
or changes?

What may happen as you start to understand this is that you become
aware of how much of what you do every day—how much of how you
react, respond, and accept or reject—is based on social conditioning.
Much is preprogrammed reflex action based on what we have been

taught, what we have seen, and what we think we know but often we are acting according to someone else's thoughts and not quite our own.

In a small way, what I have come to understand is that the first step of recognizing Hindu thought is the self-awareness that I could be wrong. What I am thinking or the way I am responding might not really be my response or might not really be what I myself think or feel; I might just be reacting in a way that I am expected to react. To reach beyond the multiple layers of my experiential conditioning—through the joys that I hold dear and the sorrows I have never entirely let go—to respond from my innermost consciousness, leaving aside the ego as far as possible, is one of the toughest things to do. But that journey starts by recognizing that all differences are man-made. The first step of that journey is melting the distinctions by liberating ourselves from the idea that there is a believer who is better and more worthy of praise and survival than an unbeliever.

The Hindu philosophical point of view is actually, in a sense, the opposite of that of monotheistic faiths. This comparison is not to suggest one is better than "the other" but just to explain the variation in worldviews. The whole business of this faith or that faith being better than another is and must be abhorrent to Hindus because if there is constantly a message of unity in all things and beings, how can there be simultaneously a competition to be superior?

Faith is just about different ways of looking at human existence and why, or whether, a sense of God is necessary. In Christianity, the starting point for all human beings is sin. Because of the original sin of Adam and Eve, every human being is assumed to be born a sinner, and salvation lies in embracing the loving message of Jesus Christ, the savior who rescues mankind from sin.

Islam believes that anything that goes against the word of Allah as revealed by the Prophet Muhammad is sin. Both these beliefs are unidirectional. In it, human beings are saved by the infinite compassion and love of the Almighty. Human beings are lost and shown the path. There is no doubt that both faiths have unique strengths—the message of the mercy of Christ and that of charity from Muhammad—but the general sense is that the human being is separate from the Almighty who rescues man.

Hinduism approaches the question of sin from exactly the other end. It begins with the idea of the perfection of man, begins with the assumption that actually there is no difference between man and God, the human and the divine, and asks how can man become even more perfect, how one can rise from *nar* to *narayan* or from merely human to divine? It says that every human has the potential to understand their own divinity and how it unites them with the universe, but usually one never discovers it. The conversation begins without a trace of the burden of sin and then goes on to place the entire onus of righteous behavior on humans.

To me, it has always seemed that sanatana dharma is telling us to stand up and take some responsibility and not leave everything to (or blame everything on) God. The karmic cycle is not about letting go and being defeatist but about taking responsibility for your actions, realizing that while you do have a karmic cycle, you can with exemplary action change that karma. You are, after all, divinity itself. The responsibility of the way your life shapes up lies finally in your hands. Not in the lines of your hand, but in your action. Your action shall determine your destiny and how close you get to realizing your divinity.

Reading the Vedanta always makes me remember the lines from the Irish poet Seamus Heaney,

> "The soul exceeds its circumstances." Yes.
> History not to be granted the last word
> Or the first claim . . . In the end I gathered
> From the display-case peat my staying powers,
> Told my webbed wrists to be like silver birches,
> My old uncallused hands to be young sward,
> The spade-cut skin to heal, and got restored
> By telling myself this.[3]

The soul exceeds its circumstances. Or at least it can exceed its circumstances if we set it free from the endless roll call of the immediate senses. The Hindu believes that there might or might not be a God above who is looking after us and to whom we can turn to in our darkest moments, but what we certainly, irrevocably have is ourselves. Hindu philosophy says we are the ones who have the right to not grant history the last word or the first claim. Our karma, or our history if you will, shall not voice our destiny unless we so will it. It shall not have the final say, for only we can allow it control on the voice of our life, and this is fascinating because it allows us choice without any external aid. There is no one "out there" to help us. A Hindu believes we have as much control as we want and seek, and also as much as we perhaps deserve through our actions.

I first read these lines from Heaney soon after I started writing this book. He is one of my favorite poets. How can one not admire a man who was a fierce nationalist who, to protest against being added to an anthology of British poetry wrote, "Be advised my passport's green. No glass of ours was ever raised to toast the Queen"?[4]

It was then prophetic to me that I chanced upon Heaney talking about restoring one's own history by willing the "staying powers" one further mile, another great stride; to convert the "webbed wrists" to "silver birches." What could be a more poetic way of describing the process of discovering the best within you?

There is a moral code of the universe, says Hinduism, the sanatana dharma, by which the entire universe lives and works, and it is the choice of man either to learn, appreciate, and play by it or not. Finally, there is no sin at birth, only a choice of action, the application of karma. The entire cycle of action and consequences is in the hands of man. The laws of sanatana dharma work not just for Hindus but for every living element in the universe. The universe itself, says Hinduism, has always worked on sanatana dharma or the harmonious code of balance that keeps everything functioning, and it always will. It is up to man to traverse that journey.

In this, I feel that the founding philosophy of sanatana dharma tends not to judge. It does not question what image you choose in your journey. It does not define sin, suggesting only that every action has a reaction in the wheel of time and karma of any nature always brings forth its reactions and results.

In a sense then, Hindu philosophy tries to push you into realizing that you can attain any and every physiological and psychological depth through any manner or form that you choose. What determines your success and spiritual elevation is your determination, your devotion to your chosen path. It chooses neither to tell you how to live or worship, nor suggests that any path you take is necessarily good or bad. It asks only that you be self-aware and responsible for your actions. In your actions, it suggests, lies your liberation.

"We do not say that ours is the only way to salvation,"[5] said Vivekananda. "Perfection can be had by everybody, and what is the proof? Because we see the holiest of men in all countries, good men and women everywhere, whether born in our faith or not. Therefore it cannot be held that ours is the only way to salvation."

One of Hinduism's greatest achievements is this recognition that our way is not the only way. This lack of theological arrogance must be the bedrock of any modern thinking about the place of God in our lives. The Vedanta philosophy is "perfectly impersonal," said Vivekananda. "It does not build itself around one man. Yet, it has nothing to say against philosophies that do; there is no fight and no antagonism."[6]

"We have no theory of evil. We call it ignorance,"[7] said Vivekananda.

This nonjudgmental, nondiscriminating approach is also incredibly important in an age when we are less sure than ever about ourselves, about where we can find love (if at all), and whether we can, possibly, be happy. These are the pivotal inner questions—as opposed to outer questions like climate change—of our time.

And we are asking those questions, aren't we? Even when we think we are not. Even when we think we are otherwise occupied, when we imagine that they do not matter, or when they are not practical, not commonsensical, not relevant, we are asking. The search for relevance, the need to evaluate every conversation and interaction and gauge the return on investment in each emotion—are these keeping us away from honestly answering the questions that emanate from us?

Notice that the phrases "stop to think" or "stop to ask a question" both start with the word "stop." It is only by ceasing our relentless daily pursuits, even with regard to language and conversation, that we can hope to get close to finding answers about who we are. It is when we stop filling silences with meaningless, escapist action that the answers start to emerge. That is the lesson of the Vedanta. This search is universal. You do not need to be a believer in sanatana dharma or call yourself a Hindu to recognize this search. You and I already know that there is something. Perhaps we sometimes struggle to define what we are seeking, yet silence eludes us. Little wonder, then, that when I entered the phrase "search for silence" on Google, it generated nearly eight million responses in less than forty seconds.

Dayanand Saraswati, the great yogic master and ascetic, spoke about the silent self, a state of consciousness wherein you realize that you are not the thoughts you have. It is because we do not understand this, said Saraswati, that we are chained to our thoughts. We are happy when our thoughts are happy, aggrieved when they are sad. This is why we rise so effortlessly to anger and give in so soon to jealousy. If the mind is restless, we are restless. The mind will always change. That is its nature, says Saraswati. But our goal is to see ourselves, not without our thoughts, but beyond or in spite of our thoughts. This, he said, was his definition of meditation. "What is the unchanging 'I' that is to be seen in spite of thoughts?" asks Saraswati. "That 'I' is silence. That 'I' is happiness. That 'I' is fullness. That 'I' is freedom. It lacks nothing. It is always free, the free, silent self."[8]

The American writer George Prochnik, who pondered his cherished moments at an ashram, called urgently for "a moment of silence in memory of silence"[9] in his book *In Pursuit of Silence: Listening for Meaning in a World of Noise*. We have to rediscover "why quiet is distinguished, or there will be no distinction between noise and signal left."

For years, my personal quarrel with the commonly seen mass version of Hinduism has been how bereft of silence it is. I live in the city of Delhi where, inevitably, someone or other organizes a *jagran* (a raucous

all-night devotional singing program almost always broadcast on loudspeakers) in the neighborhood. For an evening the night sky fills with,
usually, the most tuneless singing of praises to Sherawali Maa, a form of
goddess Durga worship. Used to the grave morning *aarti* incantation of
Durga Puja, the ten-day goddess-worship festivities of Bengal, I have
found it impossible to reconcile to these, which to my ear sound bur-
lesque, especially since many of the tunes of the songs or hymns, if you
will, have been lifted from Bollywood chartbusters with only the words
changed. (The lyrics to one recent song that I heard while I was writing
this book were *"Kal raat mata ka mujhe email aaya hai. Mata ne mujhko
Facebook pe bulaya hai"* which means "Last night I got an email from
the Mother. She has invited me to Facebook." I couldn't figure out if it
was a parody of a parody.) Researchers at the World Health Organization (WHO) are increasingly worried about the sound pollution people
are exposed to all the time—especially with the prevalence of high-
decibel headphones—and they recommend that people listen to music
for only about one hour a day. Promptly after this WHO announce-
ment, a music critic in England lashed out saying it was impossible to
listen to only one hour of music a day and that the real problem was the
volume and not the number of hours. Silence, clearly, will not come
easily to any of us.

With time, however, I have come to realize that in the true spirit of
Hinduism, I must learn to admire jagran singers for the passion they
bring to their search, as uneven and brusque as it seems to me. But I
still haven't stopped wondering why Hindus have so often forgotten the
need for quiet, the lesson of silence. Why have we lost the quietude
symbolic of the *rishis* (ascetics), the sages, and monks who were the
repositories of sanatana dharma? In my small, private hunt for silence, I
gave up watching television entirely, even selling off the TV set in my
room and convincing my parents to give away the two other TV sets at
home, within a month of leaving my job in news television seven years
ago. As a reporter, interview show host, and news anchor for approxi-
mately six years, I felt obliged to carry two mobile phones (what if the
battery of one were to die suddenly?) that often rang simultaneously. I

woke up every other morning with a call from the assignment desk at the TV station where I worked, and I finally felt that I needed to take a break from what professor Henry Higgins in *Pygmalion* would call "humanity's mad inhuman noise."[10]

At the time, I was not the only one feeling the urge to find some silence. Around me, more friends than ever were choosing to leave every few months for ten-day Vipassana courses, meditating for at least ten hours a day, eating barely a meal a day at Vipassana retreats without any reading, talking to anyone, watching or listening to any media, or using their mobile phones. In 2014, when Vipassana guru Satya Narayan Goenka died, it made headline news.

By 2015, the concept of "mindfulness" was on its way to becoming one of the world's biggest "trends" and an industry in its own right, with mindfulness conferences—including one organized at the Google offices in Dublin called Wisdom 2.0—and books like *Mindfulness-Based Therapy for Insomnia*, *Mindfulness Coloring Book*, and, of course, *An Idiot's Guide to Mindfulness*. So big is mindfulness that there is already a backlash against it, suggesting that it is a fad, just another cool thing to have—like an iPhone—and an escapist route for those who do not want to really face the issues in their lives. This may or may not be true, but what is undeniable is that some very deep-seated need of ours is not being met or fulfilled by the lives we lead, no matter where we live in the world. The growing crisis of the mind might have been dismissed as "problems of the rich" or "issues of the 1 percent" if it weren't for how widespread and diverse it is. It is certainly not confined to the 1 percent. More and more people around the world are realizing what Vedanta has long acknowledged—above all else, one must seek and find a sense of silent centeredness. Without that, the cacophony of living can drive you mad and often literally does. The WHO says depression is a global crisis. Loneliness is one of the most dreaded diseases of our times. It is as fearsome a health problem as smoking fifteen cigarettes a day and twice as deadly as obesity. Social isolation and the emptiness within is killing us. More people than ever claim that their closest companion is the TV set (or the mobile phone). Even the super rich are terribly unhappy. One study of people with an average net worth of $78 million reported high rates of anxiety, loneliness, and mental misery. On an average, the respondents said they needed 25 percent more money to be happy. This is why, at the University of Washington, professor David Levy has spent years on a teaching mission to bring what he calls the spirit of calligraphy to the digital age. Levy—who organizes conferences with titles such as "Information, Silence, and Sanctuary" and "Mindful Work and Technology"—argues that our constant multitasking "is a dangerous trend for society if it becomes our dominant way of living our daily lives. There's nothing wrong with split-focus for periods of time, but when we're not giving our full attention to anything, it reduces our humanity and our effectiveness."[11]

"Distraction is the only thing that consoles us for our miseries," said the seventeenth-century French philosopher Blaise Pascal, "yet it is itself the greatest of our miseries."[12] The travel writer Pico Iyer who, as mentioned earlier, today preaches the joy of sitting quietly in one place, is fond of pointing out that it was Pascal who taught that "all of man's problems come from his inability to sit quietly in a room alone."[13] Iyer also points out that the celebrated French products designer Philippe Starck does not read the papers, watches no television, and stays at a remote location as far away as possible from everyday noise. This, Starck has said, helps to keep his work original and consistently cutting-edge. To be alone, for Starck, is not to be lonely. This, then, is perhaps the greatest challenge of our time. We are never alone—isn't that the Facebook promise?—but at the same time, we are so utterly, heartbreakingly lonely much of the time. Social media created the FOMO syndrome or the incessant fear of missing out. Now there is also its brother mania, MOMO, the mystery of missing out. This, supposedly, is the anxiety caused when someone suddenly disappears from social media and creates within us the paranoid feeling that they may be out somewhere, having a better time than we are. In the aggressive world of instant solutions and acronyms, there's even a four-letter acronym to counter such angst—JOMO, that is, the joy of missing out. That there is reverse snobbery, even in the presence of what has been described as a global "loneliness epidemic," makes the dystopia complete.

American psychologist Sherry Turkle's work represents 360 degrees of this alone-lonely journey. In 1996, she appeared on the cover of *Wired* magazine as the pioneering author of the book *Life on the Screen: Identity in the Age of the Internet*. Turkle also spoke at the TED conference that year on the brave and exciting world of the Internet which, it was thought, would help people to delve deeper into who they really are using unprecedented technology, the likes of which would have been indistinguishable from magic only a generation ago. In 2012, she was back at TED with a very different message. Her talk entitled "Connected, But Alone?" summed up how technology and our increasing separation from the truths about our emotions and our minds (and souls) has placed us at a unique crossroads.

Technology, she argues, changes not only what we do but "who we are." In her view, it is changing not just the way we connect with each other but also how we connect with ourselves. It finally boils down to control, says Turkle. We now have the power to "clean up the richness and messiness"[14] of human relationships and to constantly control how we reveal ourselves. A conversation, points out Turkle, happens in real time. But we don't seem to like real time anymore. We can't control real time. We are lonely because our need for control denies us that one thing that makes life what it is—vulnerability. To live is to be vulnerable. Denied of vulnerability, our lives remain unanchored, bereft of centeredness. In her talk, a young boy tells Turkle wistfully, "One day I would like to learn how to have a conversation."[15] The psychologist points out that the boy says "one day," not today.

The words of Frieda Fromm-Reichmann, one of the pioneers in the psychoanalytic study of loneliness, haunt us. Loneliness, she said, is "such a painful, frightening experience that people will do practically everything to avoid it."[16] The doctor wrote in her book *Principles of Intensive Psychotherapy*, which has become a seminal text in "loneliness studies," that every study of the loneliness of others "touches upon our own possibility of loneliness."[17] She wrote, "We evade it and feel guilty."[18]

In one of her most famous cases, Fromm-Reichmann asked a young woman, who had fallen almost entirely silent, about how lonely she was. The patient lifted her hand with just the thumb stretched out and the four fingers folded close. "That lonely?"[19] asked the doctor softly, and slowly the patient's fingers opened.

As we jab away on our screens with our thumbs or one finger, this is what we seem to be telling ourselves and the world, "This is me; this is how lonely I am." It is an enduring image in a world that is plagued with fears of extreme religious polarization—ever more paranoid by the rise of ISIS—where, as *The Independent*'s Robert Fisk explained with dark mirth, "The Saudis are bombing Yemen because they fear the Shia Houthis are working for the Iranians. The Saudis are also bombing Isis in Iraq and the Isis in Syria. So are the United Arab Emirates. The Syrian government is bombing its enemies in Syria and the Iraqi government is also bombing its enemies in Iraq. America, France, Britain, Denmark, Holland, Australia and—believe it or not—Canada are bombing Isis in Syria and Isis in Iraq, partly on behalf of the Iraqi government (for which read Shia militias) but absolutely not on behalf of the Syrian government."[20]

And so the paradox of our world is that it is simultaneously lonelier and more discriminatory, more interconnected and interwoven than ever. Perhaps never before has it been more vital to discover who we truly are and how that relates to everyone around us. We are in search of a theory that connects the innermost recesses of our minds with the web of society in which we are trapped. We constantly question where we fit into all of this and what it makes of us.

To borrow from science, we are looking for the "Theory of Everything" of the mind, even as physicists try to discover the "Theory of Everything" of the universe. We are hunting for one idea that flows through everything—our fears, doubts, experiences, apprehensions, needs, wants, and every human interaction. As the *Mundaka Upanishad* says, "What is that by [the] knowing [of] which everything in this universe is known?"[21] That is the answer that Hindu philosophy seeks to provide.

Hinduism argues that the first step towards finding a cohesive answer must begin with breaking away from discrimination. It says that the search for God is really the search for ourselves; we are what we are looking for. It explains that our loneliness comes from a fundamental disconnect even with ourselves, and that is why we are failing to connect with the people around us. As we "shortchange"[22] (to use Sherry Turkle's word) ourselves of meaningful conversations, we are also willing to "dispense with people altogether."[23] And in the process, we are also dispensing with the most essential part of ourselves. Hinduism teaches that the universe is you, us. So, if you cannot converse with yourself, how can you hope to converse with the universe?

Therefore, the search for meaningful conversation within and without, the search for God and the search for our true selves, must start by dispensing with external differences. Indeed, this search is an act of peeling off layer after layer of differences. The first among them, surely, would be between people who are searching for the same thing (otherwise known as God).

Hinduism's differentiating quality, as it were, is that it starts the journey not with answers but with questions. This questioning has its roots at the very foundation of Hindu philosophy, in the Rig Veda, the first of the ancient texts.

Compare, for instance, the chapter of Genesis in the Bible and the Hymn of Creation in the Rig Veda. Both talk about how our world, the world of man, was created. Genesis says:

1. In the beginning God created the heaven and the earth.
2. And the earth was without form, and void; and darkness was upon the face of the deep. And the Spirit of God moved upon the face of the waters.
3. And God said, Let there be light: and there was light.
4. And God saw the light, that it was good: and God divided the light from the darkness.

5. And God called the light Day, and the darkness he called Night. And the evening and the morning were the first day.

6. And God said, Let there be a firmament in the midst of the waters, and let it divide the waters from the waters.

7. And God made the firmament, and divided the waters which were under the firmament from the waters which were above the firmament: and it was so.

8. And God called the firmament Heaven. And the evening and the morning were the second day.

9. And God said, Let the waters under the heaven be gathered together unto one place, and let the dry land appear: and it was so.

10. And God called the dry land Earth; and the gathering together of the waters called he Seas: and God saw that it was good.

11. And God said, Let the earth bring forth grass, the herb yielding seed, and the fruit tree yielding fruit after his kind, whose seed is in itself, upon the earth: and it was so.

12. And the earth brought forth grass, and herb yielding seed after his kind, and the tree yielding fruit, whose seed was in itself, after his kind: and God saw that it was good.

13. And the evening and the morning were the third day.

14. And God said, Let there be lights in the firmament of the heaven to divide the day from the night; and let them be for signs, and for seasons, and for days, and years:

15. And let them be for lights in the firmament of the heaven to give light upon the earth: and it was so.

16. And God made two great lights; the greater light to rule the day, and the lesser light to rule the night: he made the stars also.

17. And God set them in the firmament of the heaven to give light upon the earth,

18. And to rule over the day and over the night, and to divide the light from the darkness: and God saw that it was good.

19. And the evening and the morning were the fourth day.

20. And God said, Let the waters bring forth abundantly the moving creature that hath life, and fowl that may fly above the earth in the open firmament of heaven.

21. And God created great whales, and every living creature that moveth, which the waters brought forth abundantly, after their kind, and every winged fowl after his kind: and God saw that it was good.

22. And God blessed them, saying, Be fruitful, and multiply, and fill the waters in the seas, and let fowl multiply in the earth.

23. And the evening and the morning were the fifth day.

24. And God said, Let the earth bring forth the living creature after his kind, cattle, and creeping thing, and beast of the earth after his kind: and it was so.

25. And God made the beast of the earth after his kind, and cattle after their kind, and every thing that creepeth upon the earth after his kind: and God saw that it was good.

26. And God said, Let us make man in our image, after our likeness: and let them have dominion over the fish of the sea, and over the fowl of the air, and over the cattle, and over all the earth, and over every creeping thing that creepeth upon the earth.

27. So God created man in his own image, in the image of God created he him; male and female created he them.

28. And God blessed them, and God said unto them, Be fruitful, and multiply, and replenish the earth, and subdue it: and have dominion over the fish of the sea, and over the fowl of the air, and over every living thing that moveth upon the earth.

29. And God said, Behold, I have given you every herb bearing seed, which is upon the face of all the earth, and every tree, in the which is the fruit of a tree yielding seed; to you it shall be for meat.

30. And to every beast of the earth, and to every fowl of the air, and to every thing that creepeth upon the earth, wherein there is life, I have given every green herb for meat: and it was so.

31. And God saw every thing that he had made, and, behold, it was very good. And the evening and the morning were the sixth day. [24]

Rig Veda, "Nasadiya Sukta," The Hymn of Creation (translated by A. A. Macdonell) says:

1. Non-being then existed not nor being:

There was no air, nor sky that is beyond it.
What was concealed? Wherein? In whose protection?
And was there deep unfathomable water?

2. Death then existed not nor life immortal;
Of neither night nor day was any token.
By its inherent force the One breathed windless:
No other thing than that beyond existed.

3. Darkness there was at first by darkness hidden;
Without distinctive marks, this all was water.
That which, becoming, by the void was covered,
That One by force of heat came into being.

4. Desire entered the One in the beginning:
It was the earliest seed, of thought the product.
The sages searching in their hearts with wisdom,
Found out the bond of being in non-being.

5. Their ray extended light across the darkness:
But was the One above or was it under?
Creative force was there, and fertile power:
Below was energy, above was impulse.

6. Who knows for certain? Who shall here declare it?
Whence was it born, and whence came this creation?
The gods were born after this world's creation:
Then who can know from whence it has arisen?

7. None knoweth whence creation has arisen;
And whether he has or has not produced it;
He who surveys it in the highest heaven,
He only knows, or haply he may know not.[25]

Read the two side by side and you cannot miss the difference in tone and tenor. Genesis has answers. It is certain and doubtless. It has a sense of finality. It harbors no doubts. It is not to be challenged. It does not give a sense that there could be or might be further thought on the matter. The "Nasadiya Sukta" has more questions than answers. It leaves infinite space for future discoveries. It places those questions even ahead of the gods ("The gods were born after this world's creation").[26]

The "Nasadiya Sukta" triggers a sense of need for exploration, for discovery. It leaves the reader with a sense of anticipation that he or she alone can fulfill. Genesis, in a sense, is about the end, when humankind knows when the world began; the "Nasadiya Sukta" is about the beginning, when humankind is only starting to peel off the first layer of understanding of how the world began.

What, then, is the core difference between these two creation "myths"? Uncertainty. One embraces and revels in uncertainty, and the other structures a "truth," One sees knowledge as a journey, the other as a destination. In fact, in his celebrated book *The Wisdom of Insecurity*, theologian and philosopher Alan Watts says even Christ's message spoke of embracing uncertainty, but the message has never percolated as strongly through the ages. "This principle (of embracing uncertainty)," writes Watts, "had not been unknown to Christians, for it was implicit in the whole story and teaching of Christ. His life was from the beginning a complete acceptance and embracing of insecurity."[27]

The Vedanta celebrates this not-knowingness. This acceptance that there are always further truths to be revealed—that the truth too is a process, not a solution—is fundamental to the understanding of the Hindu view of life.

As the irascible scholar Indian writer Nirad C. Chaudhuri wrote, "Hinduism differs fundamentally from Christianity in this, that for its followers it is not an alternative to the world, but primarily the means of supporting and improving their existence in it. . . . Therefore in Hindu society every worldly activity is under the control of religion, and everything religious is involved in the world."[28] This is why the European definition of secularism is irrelevant to the Hindu. There is no singular Church to separate the State from. Chaudhuri again: "What is called for . . . is an explanation of the mingling of religion and worldly matters. Before the coming of European ideas no Hindu perceived that the two were separate things. . . . The Europeans . . . cut up life into fragments, because their method was analytical, whereas the Hindus preferred synthesis."[29]

It is because of this deeply interwoven, holistic point of view of synthesis that even atheism, a completely materialistic view of life, is part of Hindu philosophy. The Cārvāka school of philosophy in Hinduism embraces and rejoices in the material world, rejects all spirituality, and holds only that which can be experienced immediately—like reason, honesty, and action—as the basis of existence. One of the most quoted moments of Hindu spiritual encounter is a nineteenth-century conversation between Ramakrishna Paramhansa and Vivekananda—one of the first between them—which is often passed down as folklore. The young Vivekananda asks the mystic very skeptically, "Have you seen God?" Says Paramhansa, "Of course I have."

The young man is bewildered by the emphatic reply. "Where have you seen God?" he asks. "Everywhere," says the mystic. "Just the way I now see you, I see him."

"Can you show me?" asks Vivekananda.

"But of course," says Paramhansa, and with that straightforward questioning their journey begins. It is an integral part of the lesson today in the Ramakrishna Mission, the monastic order Vivekananda founded in the name of his master and whose erudite monks are known to win national awards in mathematics, that to begin the journey one must question. This act of *seeing* God is of seminal importance to Hindus. As Diana Eck has explained, Hindus go to the temple not to worship in a Western sense but for *darshan*—the act of beholding the sight of God and to be in the presence of the Almighty. "For Hindus, therefore," Eck has written, "the image is not an object at which one's vision halts, but rather a lens through which one's vision is directed. From one perspective it is perceived that there are more gods, or faces of God, than we can count . . . from another perspective, it is obvious that there is One. The fact that there may be many gods does not diminish their power or significance. Each one of the great gods may serve as a lens through which the whole may be clearly seen."[30]

The act of "seeing" or the "faculty of omniscience,"[31] explained M. M. Gopinath Kaviraj, the legendary librarian and principal of the Sanskrit College in Varansi, is conveyed in the word *pratibha*, which appears many times in the *Mahabharata*. It is the faculty through which one is able to see the entire universe and its truth clearly. In chapter 11, verse 8, of the *Bhagavad Gita*, Krishna awakens this "eye" in Arjun with the words,

> *na tu mam sakyase drastum*
> *anenaiva sva-caksusa*
> *divyam dadami te caksuh*
> *pasya me yogam aisvaram*
> For you cannot see me with the eyes that you possess,
> And so I give to you divine sight,
> So that you can see my inconceivable power.

Arjun, then, was able to see the entire universe in the immortal body of Krishna. But what did that vision show him? As Diana Eck perceived it, it showed him the oneness in many,

> *Tatray kastham jagat krtsnam pravibhaktam anekadha*
> *Apasyad devadevasya sarire pandavas tada*
> And so it was that Arjun saw the entire universe
> Divided in so many ways, but united as One,
> And as One in everything,
> In the body of Krishna, God of the Gods.

The idea of seeing means a lot to me. In my small world, I especially appreciate the interaction between Paramhansa and Vivekananda. It was what my mother spoke about when at the age of fourteen, I took *diksha*, a solemn process of pledging respect and honor to the teachings of Ramakrishna and Vivekananda. She admired the reflective, questioning attitude of this order of monks. Taking diksha means receiving a small mantra to use to meditate and focus the mind every day, preferably twice a day. After a few years of chanting , however, without any decided motive, I just stopped.

I have never been sure why. My mother tried to coax me to continue the practice because, she said, it was holy and not to be trifled with, but she knew that the impetus had to come from within; without that inner pull, the practice would be empty of meaning.

Even the idea of chanting, I realized somewhere instinctively, is robbed of its meaning unless it adds to the search. A mantra or a chant is but a method to cleanse your mind of its myriad distractions in an attempt to focus it, center it. I saw many people, including my mother, chant mantras and spend hours at temples. Peaceful when they were engrossed in that activity, they lost their calm soon afterwards, returning to the imbalance of their daily lives. Even the search for the truth, or for God, it seemed to me, had become like a fix. Once the trance was over, the meditation completed, the chanting over, the external life took over only too quickly, sometimes with increased intensity since one had taken a small break from it.

But could peace be a daily fix? Can God realization come and go via "injections" of solitude and ritual? This did not seem correct. Surely the path must continually advance us to an increasingly more centered existence? But what if the mantra itself, the process of chanting by its very nature, becomes escapist?

The philosopher Jiddu Krishnamurti questioned this too: "What is meditation? Is it to escape from the noise of the world? To have a silent mind, a quiet mind, a peaceful mind? And you practice systems, methods, to become aware and keep your thoughts under control. You sit cross-legged and repeat some mantra. I am told that the etymological meaning of that word 'mantra' is 'ponder over not-becoming.' That is one of the meanings. And it also means 'absolve, put aside all self-centered activity.' That is the real, root meaning of mantra. But we repeat, repeat, repeat, and carry on with our self-interest, our egoistic ways, and so mantra has lost its meaning. So what is meditation?"[32]

I gave up the chanting of the mantra of my diksha in part because I felt, at that time especially, that I hardly knew what I was looking for. So, what would the mantras, the chanting, center my thoughts on? The entire process of accessing the mantra, the focus on doing a round every morning and evening, and the idea that some of my relatives tried to drill in me—that this chanting would help my school-leaving board

results—seemed shallow. Surely, I reasoned with the limited understanding of spirituality I had in my teens, the purpose of the search for
God should not be something as immediate as high school exams, and
the idea that more chanting would equal better results sounded too
simplistic. I knew why I was so terrible at mathematics. It was because I
had never had the right teachers for mathematics, and, therefore, I had
never managed to develop an interest or aptitude for it. Frankly, I hated
mathematics, and unless I practiced seriously and incessantly, it was
unlikely that chanting would help me score higher marks.

There was also another thought that bothered and even irritated me.
Some of my elderly relatives tried to frighten me into keeping up the
chanting of the diksha mantra. This to me seemed stupendously silly,
even as a teenager when I had just started reading Vivekananda. How
could God, at once so vast and all encompassing, at the same time be so
utterly petulant as to sulk at one infinitesimally small me not chanting
some mantras? That made no sense.

At that time, I chanced upon a small description of Vivekananda
talking about his experience with the grammar of the Vedas. "To my
surprise," he writes, "I found that the best part of the Vedic grammar
consists only of exceptions to rules. . . . So you see what an amount of
liberty there is for anybody to write anything."[33] When I read that, it
occurred to me that an order created by a man so effortlessly analytical
and questioning would hardly bind me to a chant I did not feel connected to. I gave it up.

But my thoughts and questions about why I am Hindu and whether
God means anything to me never went away. I never stopped seeking
that knowledge, and it is only that journey and the process of trying to
discover some of those answers that propelled me to write this book. In
a sense, I had not been an ideal believer. I had taken up, on a whim
perhaps, and then given up a practice of significance. Perhaps my mind
could not be held at a place through a mantra, some chanting. My mind
was meant to follow the path of asking questions. My doubts became
my mantra, their resonant, ricocheting chant in my brain gave fuel to
my explorations, and I often wondered if all of this could be reconciled.

In his essay "The Relation of Science and Religion," Nobel Prize–winning American theoretical physicist Richard Feynman reasoned why he thought it was difficult for the scientist to reconcile with the religious believer. He postulated that a student of science has a problem of reconciling with the idea of faith in God because it usually comes with absolutism. And, said Fenyman, "it is imperative in science to doubt; it is absolutely necessary, for progress in science, to have uncertainty as a fundamental part of your inner nature."[34]

Without this doubt, this constant questioning, the scientific temperament cannot exist. That's why Feynman says that even scientists who believe in God, he thinks, have an inherently different attitude to the issue compared to other believers. "If they are consistent with their science, I think they say something like this to themselves: I am almost certain there is a God. The doubt is very small. That is quite different from saying 'I know that there is a God.'"[35]

Feynman is also worried about what he calls the "tyranny of ideas"[36] —the absolutism of religion (which he also sees in Communism)— which he argues is far away from the scientific temperament. But Feynman is clear that his reference point is only Christianity, and even in that, he admits that as far as the moral or ethical part of religion is concerned, that is largely undisputed by science because in this, as he puts it, the question is:

"Should I do this?"

And the answer in science as in the purest form of theological ethics is, "Try it and see."[37]

Feynman does not consider it, but far away from the threat of hell fire and the condemnation of the soul, Hinduism stands on a foundation of "try-it-and-see." The path here is relentlessly personal and steadfastly analytical. This is not to say that layers and layers of rituals have not been built on the philosophical edifice of Hinduism over thousands of years but that, at its core, within its collective institutional memory, the idea that anything can be reexamined and reimagined is a unique freedom.

This is why it is so difficult to find a unified "Hindu voice" even in India, where 80 percent of the population is in accordance with the nomenclature *Hindu*. The diversity of the faith is its undisputed theological strength and gives it the tensile power to absorb thousands of years of attack, invasion, occupation, and assimilation.

The Indian mythologist Devdutt Pattanaik tells a wonderful story of the world-conquering Macedonian prince Alexander on the banks of the Indus river, his gaze firmly set on his final prize—India.

There, Alexander meets a naked mendicant meditating on the banks of the river. Alexander asks the ascetic, "What are you doing?" The ascetic says, "I am experiencing nothingness."

Now the monk asks Alexander, "What are you doing?" The prince says, "I am conquering the world!"[38]

They both laugh at the futility of each other's ventures. Pattanaik uses this story to illustrate the difference between the mythologies of the East and the West. He compares the stories that Alexander and the monk would have heard. Alexander has heard about the great Greek heroes like Hercules and Theseus. He has been told that you live but once and if you live like a hero, if you win, if you conquer, then when you die, you have to cross the River Styx. If you have lived like a hero, you will be welcomed into Elysium, the heaven where heroes go.

The mendicant would have heard a different story. He would have heard of the great Bharata who also conquered the world and then climbed the great mountain Meru, hoping to be the first to put his flag on top of it. But when he reached the top, he saw it was full of flags of other conquerors—each of them believed that they would be the first there. The mendicant's view of time, or the Hindu view of time, is that of an endless loop, it is a bit like what Albert Einstein once wrote about the death of a friend, "In quitting this strange world he has once again preceded me by just a little. That doesn't mean anything. For we convinced physicists the distinction between past, present, and future is only an illusion, however persistent." The biggest difference between Hinduism and the Abrahamic faiths is perhaps in the way the two traditions look at time. For the Hindus, time is a perpetual cycle in which the present life is but a blip—and the ultimate aim is to escape from the infinite repetition of this cycle. For faiths like Islam and Christianity, time seems to be more linear—and with a definitive end in heaven or hell. This difference in the attitude towards time seems to be at the heart of structural questions, for instance, is proselytizing necessary and useful? The Hindu does not believe it is—for is it not fundamental to try and attain *mukti* or liberation from even the cycle of morality? The Muslim or Christian would perhaps say—well, if one knows and sees that people need introduction toward the "right path to god" it therefore must stand to reason that it is one's moral duty to introduce them to the correct way. There lies the difference.

The moral of the story, says Pattanaik, is that the West sees even its myths as a linear narrative, whereas the Indian viewpoint is that of an endless cycle without beginning or end. And that's what keeps our ideas of God plural, assimilatory, and ever-so-questioning and deeply individual. That's why, he points out, even the *Mahabharata* and the *Ramayana* are not two separate adventures of two different heroes but two different avatars and lifetimes of the same god, Vishnu.

But isn't there a Hindu word of God then? Couldn't there be one? Even the idea of the word of God is an individual journey, writes Indic scholar David Frawley in his foreword to pioneering researcher Ram Swarup's *The Word as Revelation: Names of Gods*. "The word of God can never be identified (in Hindu thought) with any single book or the utterance of any particular prophet, however great. It is a state of consciousness, not a written text that must be subject to misinterpretation. It is the word of truth inscribed into the heart that transcends all formulations. To discover that divine word requires individual *sadhana* or spiritual practice. It cannot come from another, from the outside, from a book, though such things can help catalyze its internal manifestation if they are approached with humility and understanding."[39]

The Hindu mind sees the inherent seamless unity in all things and, therefore, does not seek to separate the strands and distance them from one another, but rather to revel in the oneness.

5

IS GOD AFRAID OF SCIENCE?

While writing this book, Harvard-trained agricultural entrepreneur and cosmology enthusiast Ishira Mehta recommended that I consider the work of MIT scientist and theologian Alan Lightman. Lightman is the only professor ever to receive simultaneous appointments in humanities and sciences at Massachusetts Institute of Technology. In short, he is one of those rare people who straddle the world of science and religion.

He is also among a very small number of people who both agree and disagree with the gene scientist and noted God skeptic, Richard Dawkins. In the last decade, as the world has seen more and more strife in the name of God, the voice of rational atheism has been raised with much more vigor. To read Dawkins (*The God Delusion*) or the late polemical journalist Christopher Hitchens (*God is Not Great: How Religion Poisons Everything*) is to read some of the most powerful critiques of organized religion in the twenty-first century. But they have little to offer that Hinduism's fundamental philosophies have not already addressed.

Since we have referred to scientists so much in this book, let us take another example from science. Richard Dawkins, perhaps the most well-known gene biologist alive, in his now-popular book *The God Delusion*, mentions Hinduism only *twice*—only two times in a 460-page book.

The first time, he makes the observation that the polytheism of Hinduism is "monotheism in disguise."[1] This seems to indicate a fundamental and conceptual lack of understanding of Hindu theology. The terms *polytheistic* and *monotheistic* are Western constructs that arise from viewing the world through a divided lens, but the concept of monotheism in Hinduism is different than the Western interpretation of what it means to believe in one God. Hindu monotheism is a belief in one *reality* that accommodates all manifestations of that reality and does not seek to demarcate.

The second reference is merely factual. It refers to the Hindu-Muslim strife during India's partition in 1947. Basically, Dawkins's primary complaint about religion, that faith divides, is aimed at the great monotheistic faiths—Christianity, Islam and Judaism—since those faiths have clear boundaries between believers and unbelievers. For all his intellectual prowess, Dawkins does not understand that there is an alternative. He does not understand that Vedic polytheism is unique; in most polytheistic religions "the gods worshipped retain their proper and well-defined places."[2] In Vedic culture, however, "a god worshipped as the supreme deity pales into insignificance when another is adored as the highest."[3] This is the concept of the *ishta devata* by which ancient Hindus chose a manifestation of God that appealed most to them and worked to reach the highest truth through this form or image. Max Müller, the German philologist and Orientalist, called this *henotheism* (worship of one God while accepting the existence of others) or *kathenotheism* (the worship of one god at a time). It is probably neither. The best explanation comes from Surendranath Dasgupta—author of the five-volume *A History of Indian Philosophy*—who says it is neither, and that it represents an intermediary state that derives qualities from both polytheism and monotheism, yet retains a unique individualistic fluidity.

Lightman understands this. He grasps that this debate does not need to be so polarized, at least at a philosophical level. Lightman agrees wholeheartedly with Dawkins on the gene biologist's rebuttal of the theory of "intelligent design" which suggests that there might be a supernatural hand in the creation of the universe. But he disagrees with Dawkins's absolute rejection of all faith systems.

Here's the interesting thing. Dawkins came to his absolutist position as a result of those two planes crashing into the World Trade Center on 9/11. "Many of us," Dawkins has said, "saw religion as harmless nonsense. Beliefs might lack all supporting evidence but, we thought, if people needed a crutch for consolation, where's the harm? September 11 changed all that."[4]

Dawkins's reaction has come from the extreme positions taken in one religion, which have become overarching, rigid critique. The Hindu position actually resonates with Lightman's point of view in this debate. Lightman argues that while there is absolutely no reason to support an unscientific fact or theory about anything that can or ought to be proved scientifically, there are also, in our world, many things that science cannot prove.

Dawkins, objects Lightman, "seems to label people of faith as nonthinkers." "Consider the verses of the *Gitanjali*, the Messiah, the mosque of Alhambra, the paintings on the ceiling of the Sistine Chapel. Should we take to task Tagore and Handel, Sultan Yusuf and Michelangelo for not thinking?" asks Lightman.

"Should we label as non-thinkers Abraham Lincoln, Mahatma Gandhi, and Nelson Mandela because of their religious beliefs, because of their faith in some things that cannot be proved?"[5]

Lightman concludes that faith is not just about believing in God or negating scientific evidence, but about "the willingness to give ourselves over, at times, to things we do not fully understand."[6]

Any close reading of Hindu texts would agree with this. It is difficult for a Hindu to understand any inherent conflict with science. After all, the Renaissance in India was led by reformed Hindus (including several members of the family of Rabindranath Tagore, the first non-European winner of the Nobel Prize in Literature) who fought against the worst dogmatic rituals of Hinduism.

Hinduism's lack of textual rigidity has meant that its ritualistic practice can and has been constantly challenged, and its decentralized form of worship has prevented corrupt clergy or those with politically vested interests from declaring what is "true" Hinduism and what is "false." There is no parallel in Hinduism, for instance, to the inquisition of Galileo Galilei—no denial of a proper burial in consecrated ground for saying that the earth rotated around the sun and no prohibition of books such as his *Dialogues* faced for more than two hundred years. When I was in school in the late 1990s, we used to sing a song on Charles Darwin and his theory of evolution during chapel service. It went like this: "Did Charlie make a monkey out of you? / Do you think you could live in a zoo?" This was curious because we studied the theory of evolution in our science lessons, but inside the chapel, in the balmy Calcutta of the 1990s, a bit of Darwin denialism was still alive. It seemed like brainwashing propaganda, spread through the popular cultural medium of nursery rhymes for children.

But when I once asked my father about what Hindus thought about Darwin, he said without a pause, "What's the problem? Aren't there monkeys who are like men in the *Ramayana*? See? We have no problem with Darwin."

It was a joke, but the message was that Hindu philosophy had never been intimidated by science. Vivekananda, an admirer of Nikola Tesla and Darwin, even said there was a scientific approach to religion: "All science has its particular methods; so has the science of religion. It has more methods also, because it has more material to work upon. The human mind is not homogeneous like the external world . . . one person will see most, another will hear most—so there is a predominant mental sense; and through this gate must each reach his own mind. Yet through all minds runs a unity, and there is a science which may be applied to all. This science of religion is based on the analysis of the human soul. It has no creed."[7] He also emphatically said: "Is religion to justify itself by the discoveries of reason, through which every other science justifies itself? Are the same methods of investigation, which we apply to sciences and knowledge outside, to be applied to the science of religion? In my opinion this must be so, and I am of the opinion that sooner it is done the better. If a religion is destroyed by such investigations, it was then all the time useless superstitions, and the sooner it goes the better."[8] In fact, Vivekananda argues that the scientific approach to religion that the Vedanta follows ensures that it cannot be trapped in advocating a singular path.

Vivekananda felt that religion was something personal and unique to every person. He emphasized that "The end and aim of all religions is to realise God. The greatest of all training is to worship God alone. If each man chose his own ideal and stuck to it, all religious controversy would vanish."[9]

The message I grew up with was that, in the end, anything that stifled individuality and forced comformity could not be good or sustainable, and that science was not the enemy. Here's Vivekananda embracing the theory of evolution, for instance, "If we have a soul, so have they [animals], and if they have none, neither have we. It is absurd to say that man alone has a soul and the animals none. I have seen men worse than animals. The human soul has sojourned in lower or higher forms, migrating from one to another."[10]

Vivekananda was not alone in understanding this. C. Rajagopalachari, one of India's foremost thinkers, saw the Vedanta as "a philosophy of evolution." He saw that the Vedanta fundamentally understood that "the destiny of all things is change—never for an instant does anything in nature stand still." So much so that Vedanta philosophy even stretches the idea to the metamorphoses of the human soul. "The philosophy of life for the individual soul is to march from good to better by conscious effort,"[11] Rajagopalachari wrote.

But the philosophy did not deny science. It embraced the idea that, even in spiritual evolution, free will played a vital role "without which there can be no moral responsibility."[12]

In fact, it is this embrace, indeed furthering the cause of science and providing a bridge between science and spirituality, that is a consistent theme in Vivekananda's life and work. This is what has inspired people from Romain Rolland (who won the Nobel Prize in Literature in 1915) to Harvard philosopher William James (who referred to Swami Vivekananda's teachings in his work, including the seminal *The Varieties of*

Religious Experience) to Leo Tolstoy, among many others—all of whom were influenced by the teachings of the Swami and by the life of Ramakrishna. Not long before his death, Tolstoy wrote, "It is doubtful if in this age man has ever risen above this selfless, spiritual meditation."[13]

In fact, Hindu philosophy has a long and elaborate history of engaging and imaging facts about life, which modern science has validated. The most well-known among these contributions is the decimal place value system—one of the seminal discoveries in the history of mathematics. The oldest dated document (594 CE) that has a number written in the place-value form was found in Sankheda, close to the modern western Indian city of Baroda in Gujarat.

It was the Hindu scientist Aryabhata, born in 476 CE, who gave the first approximate value of "pi" correct to four decimals (62,832/20,000 = 3.1416). Indian mathematics—both in the ancient and classical period—surpassed Greek and Roman achievements, noted B. V. Subbarayappa, the first non-Westerner to be elected president of the History of Science division of the International Union of History and Philosophy of Science. Aryabhata "knew the rules for the extraction of square and cube roots, areas of triangles and trapezium, circles, volumes of sphere and pyramid, arithmetic progression and summation of series, fractions."[14]

Subbarayappa writes about other ancient texts, "The *Yajurveda Samhita* has names of numbers up to even 10 to the power of 12 and the *Pancavimsa Brahmana* gives an account of numbers in ascending order decimal scale (from 10 to the power of 1 to 10 to the power of 12). . . . In the Classical Period, the Indians had developed terminology to express numbers as large as 10 to the power of 24 and 10 to the power of 53."[15]

The seventh-century mathematician Brahmagupta devised a formula "for the sum of *n* terms of the Arithmetic Progression of which the first term is unity and the common difference is unity."[16] With this, Brahmagupta was able to accurately devise the rules to measure the volume of a prism, the area of a cyclic quadrilateral, and the formula for the length of two diagonals of a cyclic quadrilateral. Needless to say, these are rules that are being used even today.

The other Brahmagupta discovery very commonly used today is the theory of continued fractions and the general solution in integers of indeterminate equations of the first degree. He also worked out the indeterminate equation of the second degree: $Ny + 1 = x^2$.[17]

"Brahmagupta . . . formulated a thousand years before the great Swiss mathematician Leonhard Euler (1707–1783 CE) a theorem based on indeterminate equations."[18]

Kim Plofker, an American expert on Indian mathematics, has listed some key achievements of which most Indians are either unaware or have forgotten. Apart from the decimal system, she writes that Vedic priests were using Pythagoras's theorem to build their fire altars in 800 BCE, noting that "the differential equation for the sine function, in finite difference form, was described by Indian mathematician-astronomers in the 5th century CE, and the Gregory's number series pi/4 = 1 – 1/3 + 1/5 . . . was proven using the power series for arctangent and, with ingenious summation methods, used to accurately compute pi in southwest India in the 14th century."[19]

The first startling achievements of ancient Indian mathematics, especially in geometry, are recorded in the *Sulvasutras* (about seventh or eighth century BCE) or the "rules of the thread or measuring line." The oldest among these texts, the *Baudhayana Sulvasutra*, first mentions the Pythagorean theorem—for any right triangle, the square of the length of the hypotenuse is equal to the sum of the squares of the lengths of the other two sides ($a^2 + b^2 = c^2$).

Mathematician David Mumford has said that the Pythagorean theorem "might be arguably called 'Baudhayana theorem.'"[20]

Hindu mathematicians also knew what is now known as Pascal's triangle long before European mathematicians, and called it *meru prastara*. The mathematician Pingala (third century BCE) dealt with this in detail in his *Chandas-sutra*.

Pingala and Panini (fifth century BCE) are the other pillars of ancient Indian mathematics—apart from the likes of Aryabhata, Bhaskara, and Brahmagupta. Astonishingly, Panini's immortal fame is not even as a mathematician but as the definitive Sanskrit grammarian. But he also "introduced abstract symbols to denote various subsets of letters and words that would be treated in some common way in some rules; and he produced rewrite rules that were to be applied recursively in a precise order."[21]

Mumford says, "One could say without exaggeration that he anticipated the basic ideas of modern computer science."[22]

Bhaskara II, in his famous *Siddhantasiromani*, gave the correct assessment of the division of a finite number by zero. Many of his discoveries were later rediscovered, as it were, by European mathematicians like Fermat, Euler, and Lagrange.[23]

Another mathematician Sridhara wrote the *Ganitatilaka* where he outlined a method for solving quadratic equations. Mahavira, in his *Ganitasarasangraha*, details how to work with the various uses of zero and the "summation of *n* terms of a Geometrical Progression."[24]

In India, numbers also have a philosophical meaning—as Michel Danino has pointed out—and the names of numbers suggest those deeper implications. *Shunya* or zero was also called *akasha* (space, emptiness), *ambara* (sky), *ananta* (infinite), or *purna* (complete/full), while *eka* or one was also called *atman* or *brahman* to convey the understanding of unity or indivisibility. Number 10, for instance, was *dasha* or state, after the ten avatars or dashas of Vishnu; number 3 was *tri*, as in *trisula*, the trident—Shiva's main weapon; and number 9 was *nava*, as in *Navratri*, the nine-day festivities of worshipping Durga and the nine planets. (Brahma–the Creator, Vishnu–the Preserver, and Shiva–the Destroyer make up the Hindu trinity.)[25]

The Hindu obsession with large numbers and mathematical prowess stretches to far-reaching assessments about space and time by the ancients. Cosmologist Carl Sagan, a student of the Vedanta for a large part of his life, understood that "The Hindu religion is the only one of the world's great faiths dedicated to the idea that the Cosmos itself undergoes an immense, indeed an infinite, number of deaths and rebirths. It is the only religion in which the time scales correspond, no doubt by accident, to those of modern scientific cosmology. Its cycles run from our ordinary day and night to a day and night of Brahma, 8.64 billion years long. Longer than the age of the Earth or the Sun and about half the time since the Big Bang."[26]

But how was this number arrived at? According to the astrology of Aryabhata, a *mahayuga* of 4,320,000 years had four *yugas* (1,080,000 years each). A *day* of Brahma, or the age of the universe so to speak, equals 1,000 mahayugas or 4.32 billion years. Add to that the *nights*, and it comes up to 8.64 billion.

In medicine, ancient India gave us the *Sushruta Samhita* (probably sixth century BCE), which had some of the earliest and most detailed advisories on illnesses and surgery known to man. Sushruta, the medical practitioner sometimes referred to as the father of Indian medicine, described 101 types of blunt surgical instruments and twenty kinds of sharp instruments, including "forceps, tongs, scalpels, catheters, bougies, trocare, syringes, speculums, needles, saws, scissors, lances, hooks and probes."[27]

Indian physicians of that age knew delicate procedures like laparotomy and lithotomy. They knew surgical procedures to remove cataracts from the eyes, and to perform craniotomy and anal fistula operations. "Another feat," writes Subbarayappa, "related to the joining of the lips of the wound by causing them to be bitten by ants and then cutting off the body of the ants, leaving behind the mandibles which would clamp the wound."[28]

The *Encyclopaedia Britannica* (2008) notes that the *Samhita* was the world's first medical document to identify and record leprosy as a disease. Also, Ayurveda, ever more fashionable today, is based on a simple concept which we are currently reinventing with our love for organic food and sustainable agriculture—we are what we eat. Everything from the rise of veganism to the focus on vegetarianism and the contribution of cattle consumption to global warming comes from this line of thought.

In chemistry, from dyes to alcohol to the use of mercury, one needs only to look at the writings of renowned chemist Prafulla Chandra Ray and his *History of Hindu Chemistry* or those of British scientist and historian Joseph Needham to get a sense of the breadth of early chemical knowledge in India. Ray's work on a water-soluble mercurous nitrate was hailed around the world, including publication in *Nature* in 1912 and subsequently in the *Journal of the Chemical Society*. Ray, apart from writing more than one hundred scientific papers, founded the Bengal Chemical and Pharmaceutical Works, and—inspired by famous French chemist Marcellin Berthelot's voluminous *Les origines de l'alchimie* (1885)—published his magnum opus, the two-volume *History of Hindu Chemistry* in 1902 and 1908 (one volume each in those years). Instantly hailed as a breakthrough publication, the books were praised by Berthelot himself in a review.

Needham was the first living person to hold three titles simultaneously—Fellow of the Royal Society, Fellow of the British Academy, and the Order of the Companions of Honour. Needham's seminal work defines why the East, specifically China, once had a seemingly insurmountable lead in invention and technology over the West, and why it fell behind. His work on India is equally significant, especially in revealing details about the early Indian prowess in the field of distilling alcohol.

The magic of Indian knowledge of chemistry lives on even today in the six-ton, 24-inch Iron Pillar of Delhi, which is made of 99.72 percent wrought iron and yet shows no sign of rusting after around 1,500 years. Danino has also pointed out that scholar K. V. Sarma has listed 3,473 texts of scientific discoveries from 12,244 science manuscripts that have been found in Kerala and Tamil Nadu. Only 7 percent, Sharma noted, are still in print. All understanding of India's contribution to science comes from this 7 percent.[29] Imagine if one day the entire wealth of Hindu science were discovered. What do you think it would show us?

But for all the glory of ancient Hindu expertise in science, there is much to ponder about today for the modern Hindu. While it is perfectly legitimate to be proud of this rich and diverse heritage of scientific thought, how do twenty-first-century Hindus fare in the scientific field? India might be sending the cheapest-ever Mars Mission (and many of the scientists behind the project are no doubt Hindu), but Hindu society's everyday life looks dismal.

In 2015, Hindus, who constitute about 80 percent of the Indian population still tolerate (and commit) some of the highest rates of female infanticide and feticide in the world. Each year, India loses around 3 million girls to female infanticide. In Delhi (in Delhi, no less), the gender ratio is around 866 females to 1,000 males. As the *Guardian* has reported, "While census data shows that India's overall gender ratio is improving, its child gender ratio is on the decline: between 1991 and 2011, the country's female-male gender ratio rose from 927:1,000 to 940:1,000, but its child gender ratio fell from 945:1,000 to 914:1,000."[30] Nearly 17 million children in India are married. Of these, nearly 13 million are underage girls. Six million of these are mothers. In spite of numerous governments and prime ministers publicly and constantly berating the public about this, isn't it worth thinking about and asking, what is it about our society—specifically Hindu society since that's the focus of this book and also represents most of the population—which allows such utterly vile practices to continue?

How is it that the inheritors of one of the world's greatest traditions of scientific thought cannot comprehend, many of them, that it is torturous for children to be married?

That's not all. Let us consider another statistic. In 2012, 119 women were killed across Indian states because they were branded as "witches." Between 2008 and 2014, more than 760 women have been murdered for being "witches."[31] What kind of civilizational values allow this to continue? Why is it that even cities of ancient pre-Vedic India like Mohenjodaro and Harappa had neat sewage systems but today 80 percent of all sewage in India goes untreated into water sources? Why is it that, depending upon whose statistics you are reading, there are still between 100,000 and 300,000 manual scavengers in India who carry excreta with their bare hands?[32]

Why is it that ancient Hindus hymned *asatoma sadhgamaya, tamasoma jyotirgamaya, mrityoma amritangamaya* (from untruth lead us to the truth, from darkness take us to light, from the fear of death lead us to the eternal knowledge of immortality) and yet millions of Indians have never seen electricity and India remains one of the most viscerally corrupt countries in the world?

This, to me, is the greatest challenge for modern Hindus. Understanding and appreciating the knowledge we have lost is merely step one. We must also realize how to utilize, adapt, and accommodate this near-infinite reserve of knowledge into our daily lives. The easiest thing would be to gain this knowledge in the way we usually wear Indian clothes, as occasional costumes with no relevance to our day-to-day lives. But this knowledge must not remain an occasional indulgence, to be dragged out and dusted off for some annual chest-thumping. That would keep it where it has been for centuries, at the level of vacuous rituals performed without understanding, if with gusto. The idea that dharma is the guiding principle of Hindu life, and in turn the soul of India's civilizational ethos, is not something distant and whimsically esoteric. It ought to become an everyday, lived reality.

Vivekananda wanted the Vedanta to be lived, not merely worshipped. But, the Hindu escape route to our own philosophy is what I call the "avatar syndrome." You can see this in every aspect of our national existence. The avatar syndrome begins by defining every problem as someone else's problem and then waiting for someone else to come along and fix it, preferably magically and without any effort from us—that's why we keep looking for one-person solutions. An avatar, we believe subliminally, will always appear at the moment of our worst crisis, and we will be saved through that manifestation of the godhead.

In the *Bhagavad Gita*, the hymn of ethics that is revealed to the warrior Arjuna on the battlefield of the Kurukshetra in the *Mahabharata*, the god Krishna promises,

> *Yada yada hi dharmasya Glanirva bhavathi Bharatha, Abhyuthanam adharmaysya Tadatmanam srijami aham. Praritranaya sadhunam Vinashaya cha dushkritam Dharamasansthapnaya Sambhavami yuge-yuge.* [33]

Essentially this means, whenever righteousness is threatened and the truth is in danger, I am reborn in every age to destroy evil and defend righteousness.

From Vivekananda to Mahatma Gandhi (the father of the modern Indian nation), this was read as a call to action to discover the righteousness within to battle the evil inside and outside. But most of us seem to have taken this as the ultimate philosophical and theological escape route—to the extent that we now wait for the right prime minister, as we once waited for avatars, to miraculously fix our problems.

As British historian Arnold Toynbee wrote, "At this supremely dangerous moment in human history, the only way of salvation for mankind is the Indian way—Emperor Ashok's and Mahatma Gandhi's principles of nonviolence and Sri Ramakrishna's testimony to the harmony of religions. Here we have an attitude and spirit that can make it possible for the human race to grow together into a single family—and in the Atomic age this is the only alternative to destroying ourselves."[34]

We will only truly value Hinduism's great legacy of original thought if we understand that the rebirth of the *Bhagavad Gita* is the rebirth within. We are the ones we have been waiting for—waiting for a messiah goes against the very essence of the philosophy of Hinduism.

6

HOW DO HINDU BOOKS PORTRAY GOD?

If you were to write one of the most elaborate and path-breaking books on grammar ever, what would you call it?

Panini, as mentioned earlier in this book, was a mathematician of considerable agility. Author of one of the greatest texts on language ever written, called his masterpiece on Sanskrit grammar *Asthadhyayi*, which simply means "eight chapters."

Behind that coy name, mentioning only the number of chapters, the work was (and is) a landmark achievement in the history of literature. As the Indologist and historian A. L. Basham wrote, "Panini's grammar is one of the greatest intellectual achievements of any ancient civilization, and the most detailed and scientific grammar composed before the 19th century in any part of the world."[1]

Sanskrit, largely forgotten in India today and championed in Germany—with fourteen universities teaching it—is the crowning glory of the literary achievements of Hindu civilization. It is, believed the ancient Hindus, the language of the gods (though crafted and perfected by man).

Dean Brown, American physicist and translator of the *Upanishads*, has talked in detail about how the origins of Sanskrit and many of the Western languages, including English and Greek, come from the common base that is known as the proto-Indo-European language. Linguistically, he argues, Sanskrit is closer to the West than the East (China

and Japan). There is a debate about whether this almost mythical PIE
(as the proto-Indo-European language is often called) originated in
India or elsewhere. This debate links to the old Aryan Invasion Theory
(AIT), and therefore, has never been conclusively resolved. The Aryan
Invasion Theory, now largely discredited through modern genetics, suggested that all of ancient India's philosophies and texts were brought by
white-skinned, horse-riding Aryans who invaded India and wiped out
an older culture. This theory was popular especially with the British
colonialists because it showed a continuity of white supremacy in India.
Most archeologists and genetic experts today believe that no such invasion took place, and any change in population was through many slow
and gradual processes of cross-migration and assimilation.

What *is* known is that the vast riches of Sanskrit traveled from India
to China, across Southeast Asia, Tibet, and Mongolia, and the stories of
the *Ramayana* and *Mahabharata* seeped into the cultural roots of Cam-
bodia, Sri Lanka, Indonesia, Malaysia, Laos, and many other parts of
Asia.

It was Sanskrit literature and philosophy that charmed the West
when men like William Jones, founder of the Asiatic Society whom we
met earlier in this book, exulted "that Pythagoras and Plato derived
their sublime theories from the same fountain with the sages of India."[2]

When presented with a translation of Kalidasa's play *Abhijñāna-
shākuntala (The Sign of Shakuntala)*, the German litterateur Johann
Wolfgang von Goethe was moved to write, "Wouldst thou the earth and
heaven itself in one name combine? I name thee, O Shakuntala! and all
at once is said."[3]

One of the most powerful examples of our collective memory lapse
in our own literary heritage lies in Kashmir. Does anyone think about,
or are we taught in schools, the fact that between the first and the
seventeenth century, Kashmir was one of the great centers of Sanskrit
literature, producing numerous books and treatises on philosophy, religion, and language—so much so that Kashmir in ancient India was
known as the land of Saraswati, the goddess of learning?

In economic treatises, India gave the world the definitive *Arthashastra*. The importance of Indian thought in economics is its focus on dharma—the concept that binds all that is needed for nature to function smoothly. Hinduism itself, as we have discussed, is the exploration of the eternal functioning of dharma and therefore, sanatana dharma. Thomas Trautmann, professor emeritus of history and anthropology at the University of Michigan, has detailed that the *Arthashastra* was clear that the king, for instance, did not own all the land.

The king only had a share, usually one-sixth of the produce of the land, and there was a clear division between the king's land and individual property. Economic thinker Gurcharan Das explains in his introduction to Trautmann's translation of the *Arthashastra* that the most common misunderstanding about the text is a misreading of the designation "king" or *pati/swami* to mean owner of the kingdom, whereas in Indic or more appropriately, dharmic tradition, it simply means protector.

"Ancient India, as it emerges from the normative dharma texts, seems thus to present a world quite different from that of 'Oriental Despotism,' a term that the ancient Greeks used contemptuously to refer to the states in Asia and the Middle East . . . where the king owned all and everyone was his slave,"[4] writes Das.

The *Arthashastra*, philosopher Jonardon Ganeri has shown, was also a powerful contributor to the use of reason in Indian philosophy. One of the key purposes of the *Arthashastra* was to teach *anviksiki*, the discipline of critical inquiry. Kautilya, the ascetic author of the *Arthashastra*, separated critical inquiry from mere ritualistic practice and gave it an independent standing, saying "the study of critical inquiry confers benefit on people, keeps their mind steady in adversity and in prosperity, and produces adeptness of understanding, speech and action."[5]

Ganeri compares Kautilya's idea of rationality with what the philosopher Bertrand Russell (much, much later) said about reason, that is, reason "signifies the choice of the right means to an end that you wish to achieve. It has nothing to do with the choice of ends."[6] Ganeri says Kautilya, who wrote the *Arthashastra* to teach young princes statecraft, has a similar "goal-oriented and instrumental"[7] approach. "The interest is in the reasoned way to achieve some goal, whatever that goal may be. The use of reason does not tell us for which goals one should strive for, but only how to rationally strive for them,"[8] writes Ganeri.

India's greatest contribution is perhaps its philosophical thought, and though it is impossible to do justice to the vastness of Hindu philosophy in a few pages, it is critical at this point to give a sense of its unique diversity even in the age of the Upanishads. Surendranath Dasgupta, who wrote the seminal five-volume *A History of Indian Philosophy*, considered it "the most important achievement of Indian thought" because "it indicated the point of unity amidst all the apparent diversities which the complex growth of culture over a vast area inhabited by different peoples produced."[9]

Dasgupta makes the point Diana Eck would later argue, with her idea of India and its geography being crafted by the footsteps of pilgrims, when he says that the unity of India is not to be found in "the history of foreign invasions, in the rise of independent kingdoms at different times, in the empires of this or that great monarch."[10]

This is a unique sense of nationalism and nationhood that most of the West finds difficult to comprehend, but perhaps it is the only way a country as linguistically and culturally diverse as India (with twenty-two official languages and different cultures in all its twenty-nine states) can bind itself together. Here it is important to understand the point Eck is making. Nationalism got a bad name in Europe because of the fascist movement—and rightfully so. The fear of extreme nationalism still haunts Europe today. But the ancient Hindus understood nationalism differently and modern India draws many lessons from this. Nationalism in India could not, and cannot, derive its basis from uniformity of language or culture. It cannot source its glue from commonality of region, habits, or even faith. It has been multitudinous in every way for a very long time. So it accesses its national identity through a sense of spirituality which is very difficult for most of the world to understand, especially the West where interest in religion is waning and where, due to incessant religious conflict, a religious identity is often suspect. But

India has always embraced religion as its founding glue. The ancient Hindus gave this sense of plurality because their philosophies were inherently open-ended and multifarious—this does not mean that Hinduism has not had conflicts with Islam and a few recent skirmishes with Christianity in India, but what it does overwhelmingly show is that without the diverse, questioning base that Hindu philosophy gives India, the country would have experienced far greater bloodshed and an endless history of internecine warfare instead of the interwoven tapestry of culture and history that it possesses today.

So what keeps India together? Dasgupta opines that its unity comes from "spiritual aspirations and obedience to the law of the spirit, which were regarded as superior to everything else, and it has outlived all the political changes through which India passed."[11]

Even in this, it is worth recognizing the diversity in Hindu thought. There is the championing of critical inquiry but also an underlying acceptance that some truths must be experienced and not merely analyzed, for it is only the experiencing that adds a further step to the journey.

For instance, for every mention of ritual—including sacrifice—there are also the teachings of the *Brihadaranyaka Upanishad*, which preaches meditation in its place. The *Mundaka Upanishad* declares rituals and ceremonies to be useless and unequivocally calls those trapped in rituals to be "fools dwelling in darkness."[12] By the time we arrive at the *Svetasvatara Upanishad*, the mood is more conciliatory, and the talk is that of synthesis between different approaches. The Upanishads ask "What is reality?" and then—largely—answer that it is nondualism (that is, the soul of man and God are one, merged into one universal consciousness). But that's not the only answer (even though it is the one most often referenced). There is dualism, too, with portions that distinguish between God, matter, and soul. Even that is not all. There is something called "qualified nondualism" as well, which argues that it isn't this (nondualism) or that (dualism), but actually a middle path or a position in the middle of dualism and nondualism.

Now all of these sound bewildering but consider this—not one of these positions is absolutist. These are just paths, records, and journeys encountered by past seekers of the Truth with nuances and philosophies that are available to any seeker. But to finally arrive at the Truth, each seeker's journey is unique and the answer each one finds is equally valid.

The idea here is again a focus on the individual experience in the philosophy. The urge is to focus on the uniqueness of the individual experience since, in the end, all the varied experiences lead to the same truth, though experienced differently. In the end, each newness is itself an ever-repeating cycle of the same truth.

As the *Taittiriya Upanishad* says, "Having created it out of Himself, He entered into it." Or consider the *Mundaka Upanishad* which says that from the Brahman the universe has emerged and to it, it shall return.

At the core of Hindu philosophy is the celebration of this personal experience. Without the personal, the impersonal is seen as incomplete or at least not easily attainable. Hindu philosophy is bewilderingly diverse because what ancient seers did was paint the myriad experiences without force-fitting uniformity as they realized what made the philosophical unity—the final truth as it were—more magical was the countless diverse processes and paths one could take to reach it.

The only thing that remains consistent is the ultimate truth of life, the Brahman. It changes form and has many manifestations, but it alone remains the same.

There are even multiple views about the goal of life. That varies according to the two concepts of the Brahman—transcendent (that which is above and beyond) or immanent (that which is inherent or within). What is the difference? Once again, the difference is in the journey.

The final destination is identification or unity of the Atman, the individual soul, with the ultimate truth, the Brahman. But this union can happen after death—the *Chandogya Upanishad* teaches us to pray for unity with the Brahman after death. Or as the *Brihadaranyaka*

Upanishad suggests, it can happen through the course of human life, for it is merely a rediscovery of man's essential self.

How does one get to the truth? Even in this, naturally, there is no one answer. The early Upanishads advise reflection and meditation, but the *Isha Upanishad,* like the *Bhagavad Gita*, preaches action and focuses on the role of karma, along with meditation.

What does all this multiplicity really mean then to a Hindu today? Should it only confuse us? Are we to gather that we are impossibly disunited in thought?

Not quite. The philosophical multiplicity of Hindu thought actually only further promotes the idea of accommodation, questioning, and individual processes and methodologies. It is not an excuse for being frozen in inactivity. "Fight and reason and argue, and when you have established it in your mind that this and this alone can be the truth and nothing else, do not argue anymore. The truth is now to be meditated upon,"[13] said Vivekananda.

One of the biggest questions that I grappled with for a long time was the question of action. How is it, I wondered, that there is such a strong suggestion in Hinduism that the purpose of life is to discover one's self while there is simultaneously a call to action in the *Bhagavad Gita*? Was I supposed to spend my time reflecting or working energetically?

One of the distinctions and explanations helped me try to resolve this. Think of it as four paths. Vivekananda spoke of *jnana* (knowledge) yoga, *bhakti* (devotion) yoga, *raja* (meditation) yoga, and *karma* (action) yoga—four distinct paths to attain, of course, the same spiritual truth. Basically, the whole search for a greater truth comes from two fundamental questions: Is all this (our lives as we know and lead them) for real? What happens when we die? The answer(s), no matter which way you go, is (are) always (and already) within you. You are the answer. But how do you get to the answer inside you or within you?

Jnana or knowledge is one way. Through this, you essentially gather greater and greater knowledge about the experiences that are merely a by-product of your senses—including all pleasure and pain—and the experiences that go deeper and free us from the ego of putting the "I" in everything we do and feel. For instance, one of the critical ways of recognizing this, which I try to follow during moments of intense emotion or sensation—whether anger, grief, happiness, or anything else—is to step back for a moment and understand what it is that I am really feeling.

It is not an easy thing to do, and I would be lying if I said I succeed a lot at this, but once you start doing this, you will realize that it is a matter of practice. And in a really startling sort of way, it sets you free.

It is a moment when you realize what the Vedic texts talk about; you can "see" yourself undergoing a sensation or reacting to a situation. It is a bit of an out-of-body experience, but it isn't quite as weird as that sounds. It is just a sense, at the very basic level, that a lot of what we do or how we react is based on deep-rooted conditioning. Most of our reactions are knee-jerk to the extent that they could almost be mechanized. We are just, as a reflex action, behaving the way we have been told to behave or taught to behave or have seen others behave in the past.

At some point, you may realize that it's not what you *really* feel. You are reacting the way you are almost as if you are playing a part, a role. That's when you start to comprehend how fake a lot of our existence is, with much of it driven by social expectations, pressure, and conditioning. A lot of what you are doing every day, from your job to the way you react to everyone around you, is fulfilling an expected role. It often has little to do with what you really feel.

We are all just basically faking it all the time. And faking it, the Vedanta seems to be telling us, is the worst thing we can do to ourselves. "If there is a god, we must see him. If there is a soul, we must perceive it. Otherwise it is better not to believe. It is better to be an outspoken atheist than a hypocrite,"[14] taught Vivekananda.

Jnana yoga to me is a compelling argument to try to understand what we *really* feel, to seek, as Vivekananda said, "the real . . . in the midst of this eternally changing and evanescent world." To find what the *Rig Veda* describes in a hymn to the God of Fire at a funeral pyre: "Carry him, O Fire, in your arms gently . . . carry him where the fathers live, where there is no more sorrow, where there is no more death."[15]

The major idea of jnana yoga is to gain greater knowledge of who you *really* are. What does that mean? Take the first two steps of jnana yoga—*shama* and *dama*. They talk about training the mind to internalize and the sensory organs to "center" themselves so that they can determine what one *truly* feels or is experiencing. The next natural step in this process is called *uparati*, which is the practice of not thinking about the senses and going deeper into the consciousness. This is followed by *titiksha*, which, if you think about it, would follow from not being a slave to your senses; it is the idea that no matter whether faced with happiness or sorrow, adulation or insult, one accepts and embraces it without reaction. The mind is consistently calm as if nothing happened. Then comes *shraddha* or faith, followed by *samadhana* or the exercise to constantly focus the mind on divinity and finally *mumukshutva*, the desire to be free from the ties of the world.

In all of this, the critical message is: discover your true self above the bonds of ego and the senses.

Bhakti yoga is almost simpler (but not quite). It talks about one approach to the truth—love God. Just the overwhelming power of loving God, as displayed for instance by the unlettered devotion of Ramakrishna Paramhansa, is a way in itself to the divine.

Raja yoga is the art of absolute and complete meditation. For raja yoga, "no faith or belief is necessary. Believe nothing until you find out for yourself."[16] It is the ultimate mental practice to seek out the innermost recesses of the mind and conscious. It is the final method of concentration.

All of these can give rise to the following questions: so what about work? Is the deepest Hindu practice about pacific, sedentary behavior? Where does a sense of physical movement and work come from? Does it come at all? And indeed, where does all this solemn meditation and love fit into the message of action delivered on the battlefield of Kurukshetra in the *Bhagavad Gita*?

The answer lies in karma yoga. It teaches us not to give up the world. Live in the world, it instructs, do your level best in everything that you do, but do everything without ego and without attachment. But then, comes the question, how can high-quality work happen without ego, without the desire to do better? Isn't a sense of ego the propeller of greater achievements? No, says the philosophy of karma yoga, and gives the example of the functions of the body. The body sees, but does the action of seeing, which happens effortlessly, have ego? The body digests, but is there any determined ego working behind the digestive process? When artists immerse themselves in their art, ego is lost, and often the greatest works emerge from this process.

So, karma yoga says detached action that completely absorbs the person conducting that action is the highest method or process to reach the truth. As Krishna teaches—do the work but never bother about the result. The result is not in your hands.

As a final blow to the ego, karma yoga also teaches that the notion that through good action we are helping the world is mistaken. In reality, we are only helping ourselves with our good karma. "The world does not require our help at all," wrote Vivekananda. "This world was not made that you and I should come and help it."[17] On the contrary, what we help through our actions is ourselves and not the world. Even while giving alms, teaches karma yoga, it is the giver who should be thankful that there is someone to receive his or her philanthropy, for it is the giver who earns karmic brownie points, so to speak, and not the receiver.

The world does not need our help at all. Only *we*, ourselves, need our help. The most powerful illustration of this thought, to me, is in the difference in the reform movements in Christianity and Islam, and Hinduism. After all, reformation is but a faith trying to aid or assist its own world towards a better future. The idea of reform also weighs heavily on me as I write this book, as demands for reform in Islam grow more cacophonous around the world as ISIS atrocities and Boko Haram barbarism grows, and as the Taliban returns to its extreme bombing ways.

One of the most convincing arguments I have read against a knee-jerk call for reform in Islam was written by the British journalist Mehdi Hasan. Hasan is a critic of the Somalian writer Ayaan Hirsi Ali who, having suffered many tortures and indignities in her home country from an orthodox clerical order, has called again and again for reform within Islam, asking for the faith to shed its most extreme views, including those that seem to legitimize, according to her, severe bloodshed.

Hasan, in a piece visibly seething, responds by reminding us, first, what reformation was in Christianity. He details, in case anyone has forgotten, that Martin Luther—the fourteenth-century German cleric who was the Father of Reformation—not only broke the Bible free from Latin upper class domination by translating it into vernacular languages, but also wrote *On the Jews and Their Lies* (1543). In this, Luther referred to the Jews as "the devil's people and called for the destruction of Jewish homes and synagogues."[18] The book is one of the seminal texts of German anti-Semitism, and later the Holocaust. Hasan quotes the American sociologist and Holocaust researcher Ronald Berger as saying that, for all of Luther's admirable challenges to the orthodoxy and financial impropriety of the Catholic Church, it was this German friar who "helped establish anti-Semitism as a key element of German culture and national identity."[19]

Hasan correctly asks if this is the sort of reform that Islam needs. The answer, naturally, is no. After all, it is not just Catholicism that had a troubled reform history. The Protestant Reformation was equally blood-soaked. It is easy to forget today that whether it is the English civil war or the French wars of religion or the thirty-year-long German war that killed 40 percent of the population of that country, it was all in the name of religious reformation.

Islam, too, says Hasan, has had reform. The most successful "reformist" is, even today, stamping his thought around the world. His name is Muhammad ibn Abd al-Wahhab, the father of the ultra-orthodox Wahhabism according to which Saudi Arabia is governed and which is at the core of the most fanatical Sunni-led violence around the world. It was Wahhab, the eighteenth-century purist, who bitterly critiqued the relative liberalism of Sufism and described both Jews and Christians as devil worshippers. The punishment for devil worshippers, said Wahhab, was the sword. He showed some writings of the Prophet Muhammad to justify this.

Suffice it to say that almost every Islamic extremist has drawn inspiration, in some way or the other, from Wahhab's teachings. Let us now look at the Indian example. It is not as if Islam has not had its reformist scholars in India. The most prominent, though barely mentioned these days, was Dara Shukoh. The tale of Dara is one of the most poignant in Indian history. Usually, to bring to light the synthesis that took place between Hinduism and Islam in India during the Mughal rule, the example of Akbar is considered. He was an emperor who began as a hardliner but increasingly grew more tolerant towards various faiths and even tried to bridge some of the divisions with the creation of a comprehensive spiritual ideology called *Din-i Ilahi*. But Akbar had the Mughal crown on his head and near infinite powers in his vast empire. The ability to bring radical reform was easier for the emperor whose arrival proclamation declared him as the "shadow of god on earth."[20] Shukoh, his great grandson, is a more interesting character. To understand the depth of Shukoh's grand idea, let us turn for a moment to the theologian and philosopher Jonardon Ganeri's *The Lost Age of Reason*. Ganeri chooses 1656 as a seminal year for the flowering of a culture of syncretism in India.

"In India, this was the year in which a long-running process of religious isomorphism, pioneered by Akbar's chronicler Abu-i-Fazl and orchestrated around the idea of Ibn al-Arabi, the Sufi mystic and philosopher, of 'unity in being' (*wahdat al-wujud*), reached fulfillment in Dara Shukoh's grand project to translate 52 Upanishads in Persian,"[21] writes Ganeri, professor of philosophy at New York University.

What was happening to Dara Shukoh in the year 1656? In that year, Dara Shukoh, the chosen heir to the throne of Shah Jahan—the builder of the Taj Mahal, the owner of the Peacock Throne and the Kohinoor diamond, the great Mughal who lorded over the treasures of India—began a unique experiment. He was not emperor, not even close, but he was certainly the favorite among the four sons of Shah Jahan, says the historian Jadunath Sarkar, author of the definitive four-volume *The Fall of the Mughal Empire*.[22] Dara, influenced by Sufism, had read the *Talmud*, the *New Testament* and the Vedanta. He had been a pupil under the Muslim fakir Sarmad and the Hindu yogi Laldas.

Then, he embarked on his greatest project, for which he gathered at Kashi (Benaras) a vast troupe of bilingual scholars. This for its time was unprecedented. He was forty-one years old, and his father, Shah Jahan, was sixty-six and already growing weaker, with no definite heir to the throne in sight. The emperor had to make a decision soon, and it would not have been an easy decision. Though his four sons were from the same mother—rare in the world of the sprawling harems of Mughal emperors—there was little love between them. The two strongest contenders to the throne were Dara Shukoh and the puritanical Aurangzeb. Such was the hatred between Dara and Aurangzeb that the emperor had to keep them away from one another to keep the peace.

Aurangzeb was, thus, kept far away in the south of India, fighting wars for his father and the Mughal crown, while Dara Shukoh was always by the emperor's side. The year 1656 was eventful for Aurangzeb, too. This was the year he invaded Golconda, home to some of the greatest diamond mines the world has ever known. In this battle, which Aurangzeb finally had to desert, censured by his father, Dara Shukoh took the side of the local ruler and got his father to accept a peace treaty and the payment of an indemnity. By the end of the year, while Dara was busy with his grand translation project, Aurangzeb invaded Bijapur. But again as victory seemed so close, the ruler used influence in Delhi through Dara and thwarted his plans through another stern message from the emperor.

By the end of 1657, Shah Jahan was already ill. This was when Dara Shukoh pushed his plural agenda. He knew, of course, that his greatest rival, his brother Aurangzeb, was known as a puritanical Islamist. He also knew that even though he was no apostate and "never discarded the essential dogmas of Islam," his "coquetry with Hindu philosophy made it impossible for him, even if he had the inclination, to pose as the champion of orthodox and exclusive Islam, or to summon all Muslims to his banners by proclaiming a holy war."[23] This he certainly would have recognized could well be the fatal chink in his armor against any potential rival, especially Aurangzeb.

But Dara Shukoh still continued his work of immense daring—daring because he suggested several things that few, if any, before him had suggested from the position of such influence in Islam. He brought about the idea that the *Upanishads* are hermeneutically continuous with the *Quran*, and that the *Upanishads* "are first of all heavenly books . . . in conformity with the holy *Quran*" and that the *Upanishads* are "actually mentioned in the *Quran* and designated as scriptural texts."[24]

Dara Shukoh's great book comparing Islam, as seen by the Sufis, the version that appealed to him, and the Vedanta, specifically the *Upanishads*, is the *Majma al-bahrayn* or "the meeting place of the two oceans."

Ganeri writes, "after knowing the truth of truths and ascertaining the secrets and subtleties of the true religion of the Sufis and having been endowed with this great gift, he thirsted to know the tenets of the religion of the Indian monotheists; and having had repeated intercourse and discussion with the doctors and perfect divines of this religion, who had attained the highest pitch of perfection in religious exercises, comprehension, intelligence and insight . . . did not find any difference, except verbal, in the way they sought and comprehended Truth."[25]

What did Dara Shukoh get for his troubles? His discoveries added disastrously to his downfall. Defeated in battle, it was easier for Aurangzeb to get rid of him since he could be accused of heresy. He was executed in 1659. It has been suggested that had it not been for the accusation of heresy against Islam, which could not have held if Dara had not been so pluralist, it would not have been easy for Aurangzeb to murder him. And so it came to pass that perhaps the most peaceful imperial reformist of Islam in India finally died a violent death.

Compare this with Hindu reform movements and reformists. Look for instance at the Brahmo Samaj (the nineteenth-century reformist movement in Calcutta) and its founding lights, like Raja Ram Mohun Roy, Debendranath Tagore, Pandit Ramchandra Vidyabagish, and Dwarkanath Tagore. Look at men such as Ishwar Chandra Vidyasagar and Akshay Kumar Datta. One of their key achievements was to end a form of ritual violence within Hinduism—namely, that of sati, wherein women in some parts of India were compelled to end their lives on the funeral pyres of their husbands. The suicidal pact probably first started with women preferring death to dishonor before the marauding armies that killed their husbands. It had, by the nineteenth century, become a vicious ritual used in many cases by families to deprive women of their inheritance in the name of faith. In some cases, women were heavily drugged before being literally flung onto the pyre. Such cases were well known enough to have popped up in English adventure stories of the late nineteenth century. In Jules Verne's *Around the World in Eighty Days* (1873), the imperturbable Phileas Fogg saves the beautiful Aouda, who is drugged and about to be sati-ed.

Campaigning fervently with the British government, the Brahmo Samaj and reform-minded Hindu religious leaders, such as Sahajanand Swami, the founder of the Swaminarayan sect (today often described as the wealthiest Hindu group in the world), got sati banned through William Bentinck, the Governor-General of Bengal, in 1829.

Another, even more notable example is that of B. R. Ambedkar who fiercely denounced the orthodox Hindu caste system which kept many people of the lower castes trapped near slavery. Ambedkar, born into a lower-caste family, rose to become an ardent scholar and eventually authored the constitution of modern India. He argued acerbically with even Mahatma Gandhi regarding caste (and was often more realistic about the discrimination on the ground than Gandhi was); he used the power of the pen all his life to campaign against the caste system. As a final blow against caste, barely weeks before his death, he held a mass conversion ceremony of nearly 500,000 lower-caste Hindus to Buddhism. He had by then converted to Buddhism himself and, by the time of his death, had also completed the masterly *The Buddha and His Dhamma* (1957).

What is striking in these examples is the lack of violence in the major reform initiatives within Hinduism. Vivekananda's idea that it is not the world but we ourselves who need assistance resonates in Hindu reform movements as their trajectory is inward-facing, and perhaps that is one of the reasons why they have never turned to major violence.

As we saw, even in the four kinds of yoga there is no one way to reach the same truth. That's because the goal is always the same—to discover for yourself *tat tvam asi* (you are that).

Surely, the idea that you already have "the word of God" in you, that you were born with it and merely have to rediscover it within yourself is an incredibly powerful and liberating one.

By the way, before we end this chapter on words and God and the intermingling of the two, let us not forget that not all words and texts that came from Hindu civilization are solemn or philosophical. Sometimes, instead of seeking the highest elevations of the mind, they seek the unabashed pleasures of the body.

An interesting thing that is rarely mentioned with regard to the *Kamasutra* is that it was actually one among many such books written at a unique time when Hindu society was lush with sexual advice notes, and was probably presented in the form that we know today sometime in the second century. Apart from the *Kamasutra*, there was the *Ratirahasya* (or "the secrets of love"), the *Ratimanjari* (or "the garland of love"), the *Rasmanjari* (or "the sprout of love"), and the *Panchasakya* ("the five arrows"), among others. Books like these were usually written by poets. The man who wrote *Panchasakya* is Jyotirisha, not only a great poet but also one of the finest teachers of music. *Ratirahasya* was written by a poet called Kukkoka.

For a moment, let's imagine the time when the *Kamasutra* as we know it today is being put together. As the Pax Romana is ending in Europe, the last of the five good emperors is dead with the passing of Marcus Aurelius; Indian civilization is flourishing and prosperous, so much so that books like the *Kamasutra*, devoted to the celebration of the senses, are being written—books that are neatly categorizing men based on the size of their penis as "hare man," "bull man," and "horse man," and women based on the depth of their vagina as "female deer," "mare," or "female elephant."

What is the kind of devotion to sensuality in a civilization that it can come up with and describe in detail and with care not one or two but sixty-four positions of copulation? But a variety of positions is not the only thing that is so interesting about the *Kamasutra*, though, of course, that is the most discussed. It is a text that has the emotional intelligence enough to understand and define four kinds of love.

There is love acquired by continual habit, love driven by the imagination, love resulting from belief, and love that is caused from the perception of external objects. The most insightful thing here is that it distinguishes the love that comes from regular interaction, like the intimacy born of regular sexual intercourse, from the love "from belief" which it says is mutual and comes from a feeling that the two people "belong to one another."

It is this intricacy of emotional detail, this unraveling of the psyche that defines most Hindu civilizational texts and makes them relevant and enjoyable even today. This perhaps has helped to maintain their longevity. How sublime that they were able to, even then, put some soul into the carnal.

7

ARE ALL HINDUS VEGETARIANS?

Are all Hindus meant to be vegetarians? This is a question that often crops up, usually in the context of eating or not eating beef. Is Hinduism a religion of vegetarians?

For all the controversy, there are actually simple answers to this question.

What constitutes our search for God? If you don't want to call it God, call it what you will, but what makes up that search?

Vivekananda says that, in that search, Hindus often forget the main lesson of their own faith—the unity and divinity in all things and the search for truth within—and instead, persistently focus on the absurdly peripheral. Interestingly, Swami Vivekananda, the greatest modern monk of the faith, was not a vegetarian. As we shall see, that is not even the main point.

In fact, rarely has a seer been as harsh in exposing the inanities of meaningless Hindu rituals as Vivekananda. Here, speaking to citizens of Shivaganga and Manamadurai, he says, "Give up all those old discussions, old fights about things which are meaningless, which are nonsensical in their very nature."[1]

This sets the tone for what is to come. Remember, this is a monk speaking to an essentially orthodox populace in nineteenth-century, British-ruled India, a people dogged by centuries of ritualism. He is speaking to Hindus less than seventy years after sati has been banned.

To them, an ascetic in his thirties is saying, "Think of the last six hundred or seven hundred years of degradation when grown-up men by hundreds have been discussing for years whether we should drink a glass of water with the right hand or the left, whether the hand should be washed three times or four times, whether we should gargle five or six times. What can you expect from men who pass their lives in discussing such momentous questions as these and writing most learned philosophies on them? There is a danger of our religion getting into the kitchen. We are neither Vedantists, most of us now, nor Pauranics, nor Tantrics. We are just 'Don't touchists.' Our religion is the kitchen. Our god is the cooking pot, and our religion is, 'Don't touch me, I am holy.' If this goes on for another century, every one of us will be in a lunatic asylum."[2]

Search carefully the annals of theology and rarely will you come across a more stark and uncompromising strike at mindless orthodoxy. Vivekananda is, for this, the ultimate modernist in Hinduism. He not so much pushed but dragged Hinduism into the future and forced it to face its deepest, most resonant lessons, brutally tearing apart the lulling façade of endless ritualism.

Why only Vivekananda? Read Gandhi, perhaps the greatest supporter of cow protection and the most powerful voice against cow slaughter, on vegetarianism. What is Gandhi saying? "Unfortunately today Hinduism seems to consist merely in eating and not eating. Hinduism is in danger of losing its substance if it resolves itself into a matter of elaborate rules as to what and with whom to eat. Abstemiousness from intoxicating drinks and drugs, and from all kinds of foods, especially meat, is undoubtedly a great aid to the evolution of the spirit, but it is by no means an end in itself. Many a man eating meat . . . but living in the fear of god is nearer his freedom than a man religiously abstaining from meat . . . but blaspheming god in every one of his acts."[3]

The argument that the Hindu mind is enfeebled by centuries of shallow routines resonates even today. The point is not, per se, what we eat, or wear, or how many times we go to the temple or on which day of which week we fast; none of this is relevant. These rituals might be useful for someone as the first access points to spirituality, but they are not core in any way. They are not core to the philosophical search of Hinduism. They do not add any intrinsic value to the spiritual journey of the soul and at best, might be useful tools or entry-point crutches. They are not relevant or illuminating in the greater scheme of things. They are, if we remain enmeshed only in them, as Vivekananda said, "a sure sign of softening of the brain when the mind cannot grasp the higher problems of life."[4]

To think of the theological debate on Hinduism as an argument for or against cow slaughter is facile and redundant. The heart of the Vedanta does not lie in cattle.

How then should we look at cow slaughter? Perhaps the reasonable thing to do is to see it for what it is. First, accept that in the early part of our ancient history there were instances of eating the meat of buffaloes (and perhaps sometimes cows). As Vivekananda writes, "There was a time in this very India when, without eating beef, no Brahmin could remain a Brahmin."[5]

Vivekananda was clear about this. He explained that a distinction needs to be made between the timeless philosophies of the Vedas and other rules or laws based on the local customs of an era, or what he termed *Smritis*, which change with the times—"other *Smritis* will come."[6] This is what makes Hinduism ever contemporary. Without this flexibility, the faith would become rigid and collapse. The practical idea that seems to have evolved from that point in history is that meat, more than anything else—food that produces heat in the body—is perhaps best avoided for the mind and the body to remain cool and calm. Also, the sedentary, meditative existence of the Vedantist, steadfastly sitting and focusing on the innermost recesses of the mind and soul, is not quite the right lifestyle for calorific, heavy meat eating.

The point here is that food is just that. While it is important for the body, it has only that much of a role in the spiritual path. Also, as Vivekananda mentions, the arrival of the Buddha and his teaching of nonviolence further moved public consciousness away from cow slaughter. There was also a realization, according to the Swami, that "we were an agricultural race . . . therefore the practice was stopped, and a voice was raised against the killing of cows."

Vivekananda makes a clear distinction between two things in religion—one which is eternal and another which has a time-bound, limited purpose. Of Vivekananda's teachings, this is one point that has been, and ought to be, ever pertinent. It talks about the existential challenge of Hindu civilization, the raison d'être of India, that intricate and delicate balance between timeless lessons and everyday nuances, wisdom and information, the vast and the infinitesimal, customs and God realization. "Various are the customs all over India, but they are local. The greatest mistake is that ignorant people always think that this local custom is the essence of our religion,"[7] said Vivekananda.

A custom then is merely a methodology, a thought that is a path to the truth but cannot be seen as separate from the truth. And once the higher levels of intellect are achieved, customs metamorphose and are even shed.

Think of the conversation between the Hindu mystic Ramana Maharshi and a Jesuit priest.

Priest: I come from God. Isn't God distinct from me?

Maharishi: Who asks this question? God does not. You do. So find out who you are, and then you may find out whether God is distinct from you.

Priest: But God is perfect and I am imperfect. How can I ever know him fully?

Maharishi: God does not say so. It is you who ask the question. After finding out who you are, you may know what God is.[8]

With regard to vegetarianism or nonvegetarianism, there isn't one right way. It is just food. As Vivekananda taught, meat is suitable especially if the person who is eating it is doing hard, physical labor. Eating light is better for more sedentary lifestyles. This much is basic common sense (and is also supported by medical science). It has little to do with how progressive or regressive Hindus are. Progressiveness is the ideal and the goal, but it can only be achieved with respect for traditions. However, those traditions have to keep evolving, not just in society but also step by step in your private journey. Perhaps, to start with, you need a temple, an idol, and daily rituals, but as you move ahead, you might realize that you don't need these things. They are but crutches.

Vivekananda—and the Vedanta—do not offer platitudes about "letting go" of crutches. The message here is more unique. It says enjoy, even revel in, your crutches, aids, assistances, idols, rituals, call them what you will. That, too, is part of your journey, and indeed a crucial part; at least you are searching. But as you do so, take care to recognize that the magic is not in your method, even though it might seem magical to you. Even meditation itself can become a crutch, a respite from engaging with the self and the world, an escape route.

So, there is a broader societal consensus among most Hindus that cow slaughter is best avoided, but there is a much bigger point to be addressed about how Hindus look at nature. Conceptually, this cannot be confined to mere vegetarianism. This is about how a civilization approaches the environment and what Hindu traditions regarding the environment are particularly relevant today.

The sage Manu, who wrote the book of social guidance for Hindus, the *Manusmriti*, said "don't spit in the waters of a river" (or any other water body for that matter). Today, India's Central Pollution Control Board says half of the country's rivers are officially declared as polluted. As it happens, the number of polluted rivers in India has doubled in the last five years, rising from 125 to 275. So unclean is the Ganga, the holiest river for the Hindus, that it barely deserves reverence anymore. The Yamuna, the other great holy river, is little more than a drain these days. After decades of spending millions of dollars on so-called Clean Ganga (and Yamuna) mission plans, the present Indian government is making a renewed thrust at cleaning the river, with a centralized fund of $3 billion. One hundred towns along the course of the mighty river will be the focus of this cleanup. The idea is that the waters of the Ganga, even at its most crowded pilgrimage spots, must seem sparkling and pristine. But is cleaning the river—as vastly important as it is for India's ecology and spiritual harmony—enough?

While writing this book, I spent a few days in Benaras (Kashi/Varanasi). Deciding to go to Benaras was fixed in my mind. I was a boy, three, maybe four, when two of my grandparents died within a fairly short period of time. I remember my father and his brothers taking the train from Calcutta to Benaras, twice, to immerse the ashes of my grandparents in the Ganga there. Stuck in a hazy corner of memory is a relative, I cannot recall who, saying that they (my grandparents) could not die in Banaras—the second, newer name for this holiest of holy towns—but that they deserved at least to have their ashes drowned in the Ganga. I specifically remember the word "drowned." It had, even then, seemed ill-fitting to me that it was used for those who had just died, and died, as it so happened, not from drowning.

I have memories of my father leaving the Howrah railway station with the ashes, and of my uncles, their heads shaved clean, wearing open shirts and trousers for the first time in days (as they had changed into white unstitched cloth and, shunning shoes, walked around in rubber slippers immediately following the deaths).

Each time, I was too young to go along, so I stayed back in Calcutta, at home, unsure about this new idea—death. The whole notion of setting off to drop ashes in a river seemed vaguely adventurous. Ever since then, I've had a sense of excitable, fearful anticipation about the place, akin to the feeling you get when you know you are about to find out something that won't let you be the same you. You know that a new awareness is coming. You are even afraid of it, not because you want to be, but because it is the right thing to do. That was my memory of Benaras. I had, it would be fair to say, no memory of Kashi, the ancient Indian name of the holy town, or its colonial nomenclature Varanasi.

Thirty years later, when I decided to go to Benaras, it called up underlying memories of my first knowledge about death. I finally went to the city the year that my father turned seventy and my mother sixty-five. My grandparents, on either side, had mostly not made it to this age. Only my mother's father, my *dadu*, had lived to be eighty. I had little recollection of my mother's parents; I must have been around ten when they died. What did I know of Benaras, then, but death? What did I know of Kashi, the spot where creation began, says the Hindu faith, the city of Shiva himself?

I went to Benaras with Diana Eck's 1983 classic *Banaras: The City of Life*. She had first seen Benaras as a student fifteen years before she wrote the book. She had studied in the city for a year and then, enamored of it, returned again and again. In the book, she "saw" the city through Western eyes and also quoted extensively from various European travelers who had been both intoxicated and repelled by its chaos, but she also viewed it through Hindu eyes, seeing and revealing the construction of the palimpsest. She reads the *Aitareya Brahmana* where Indra, king of the gods and "protector of travelers," urges a young man, "There is no happiness for him who does not travel. Therefore, wander!"[9]

Eck sees that Hindus have embraced this wanderlust, often as pilgrims, and in Benaras, the pilgrims find "everything on earth that is powerful and auspicious . . . all the gods reside here . . . all of the eight directions of the compass originated here . . . all of time is here."

I tried hard to see all that in Benaras, but it was very difficult. Uttar Pradesh interrupted me at every step. I saw, to begin with, what one would expect in one of India's most dysfunctional states—a crumbling, corrupt place with 200 million people. The drive from the airport to the hotel was spine-wracking, the roads broken or absent, and traffic rules at best whimsical. Benaras town was so crowded that it felt bitter. Still, there was some leftover anticipation for me—after all, Benaras was the parliamentary constituency of the new prime minister. There was much talk of some ghats, the famed bathing steps of the city, getting cleaned since Narendra Modi had won the election. Those ghats, my driver told me, had not been cleaned since the days of Shiva. He laughed sadly. Benaras, said my driver, could defeat the best-meaning prime minister.

In the middle of the afternoon, I tried going to the Kashi Vishwanath temple, the most sacred of the Shiva shrines in Benaras. I had been told that this was a relatively good time to go there. When I arrived half a kilometer away, beyond which the car could not go because there were too many people, my driver said this seemed like a good day, seemed like I might not have to stand too long in a queue.

Imagine the most crowded place you have ever seen. More people and more loudspeakers than you have ever seen, and then imagine ten times that—*that's* what the shrine looked like. Policemen with flailing arms, stained collars, and plastic whistles in their mouths were pretending to guide the crowds. They had a use. They were telling everyone who passed them by to be careful of pickpockets. The loudspeakers, now and again, took a break from the incomprehensible Bollywood-style devotional songs and warned the same, that there were pickpockets everywhere. "Be careful. Shiva won't protect your wallet."

To reach the Kashi Vishwanath temple, after passing through endless streams of people, one enters a lane lined with shops on either side. What are they selling? Blind faith—overpriced sweets, greasy floral garlands, a little cane basket to carry it all. Also, there was a special charge at every shop to keep your shoes safe in little grubby shelves or iron safes—a package deal where you can buy offerings for the holiest Shiva in Benaras and keep your shoes, as well as get a small discount if you bargain hard.

Not one shopkeeper waits for you to approach them. Instead, they lean into the pathway, one foot inside their stall, and try to wave you in, or even grab you with the logic that "Your shoes are as safe here as there, and the tray the same, so why not my shop instead of his?"

Between the pickpocket warning and the escape-the-shopkeeper obstacle course, I felt compelled to worry more about my wallet than to ponder the mysteries of Shiva.

The queue was long but not that long, only half an hour. During this time, parents carrying bawling children spoke excitedly all around. The archways were small. The building, encroached upon by shops and other haphazard construction, was dimly lit, ancient smelling, and inadequately ventilated for even the lung power of two-year-olds.

When the queue started moving, it all happened very rapidly. In the *garba griha*, the sanctum sanctorum where you can maybe get, if you are lucky, a five-second glimpse of the Shiva linga and pour milk on it, you feel like a stampede might start any moment.

As you rush out of the claustrophobic tunnels, with shopkeepers still doing their snatch-and-grab routine, the overwhelming sense is of relief. Says the *Atharva Veda*: "Let there be peace in the heavens, the earth, the atmosphere, the water, the herbs, the vegetation, among the divine beings in Brahman, the absolute reality. Let everything be at peace and in peace. Only then will we find peace."[10]

But there is no peace to be found in most Hindu temples. At the slightly less crowded shrine of the fierce Kal Bhairav, the protector of Kashi, the sanctum sanctorum had a very fat priest sitting next to the idol in a flaming red dhoti. Even before I could properly bow before the idol, he proceeded to tell me the rates of the various *pujas*—some to get wealthy, some for conceiving a child—which I could pay for. When I escaped this "puja à la carte" menu and went to see the famed Ganga *aarti*, the salutations with oil lamps to the river in the evening, there were young priests asking the crowd to wave their hands and clap with the music in the beautiful ceremony of the lamps lighting up all of the ghats and the boats in the river. In their hands, though, the priests held up CDs of the songs of the aarti and DVDs of the ceremony. Every now and then, there was a quick line in between the aarti, urging people to buy the CDs and the DVDs. There was no fleeing commerce in Kashi.

This is something that modern Hindus might want to consider. Why are our places of worship so often disgracefully dirty and disturbingly malodorous, with petty cash transactions going on rather than practices that provide some solace for the soul? Why are people who profess to live by a faith that consistently talks about the manifestation of God in nature seemingly unable or unwilling to keep their holiest places clean?

Think about this: for thousands of years, we have been worshipping the sun, and yet we have been one of the least enthusiastic countries with regard to using solar energy to replace fossil fuels, even though we have been blessed with enormous solar capacities.

One of the most well-known parts of yoga is the Surya Namaskar or the sun salutation—but for years no one paid any attention to the mass use of solar energy in India. (That thankfully seems to be changing as India has pushed for one of the biggest solar energy use programs in the world in recent years.)

In every bit of our religious texts, the worship of water and the reverence for rivers is embedded, and yet India has some of the dirtiest rivers in the world. We seem only too happy to simultaneously pollute that which we worship.

How does that even make sense?

The earth is considered the Devi, the bountiful mother goddess, in the Hindu faith and yet such is our concern for the earth that large parts of India have some of the most toxically polluted soil in the world. Soil contamination levels in Punjab, the "food basket" of India, are such that doctors there now call it the "disease basket." In almost every area where food is grown, there is now a groundwater shortage crisis and a sense that food cultivation is deeply threatened throughout India.

Does any of this suggest a civilization whose cornerstone is respect for nature? It doesn't. As a Hindu this is, and indeed ought to be, one of my fundamental questions today.

8

HOW DO HINDUS CONSIDER THEIR OWN HISTORY?

If everything, I was once asked, is cyclic and repetitive in the Hindu worldview, then what about history? Why this specific concern with history? This is because Hindus have had a bit of an issue with history. Unlike, say, Islam and Christianity, which have meticulously written down their history as they have seen it through the ages, Hinduism sometimes relies on collective memory, mythical references, and parable references to put together historical timelines. It is not that the Hindus did not write their history—they did. But because the timeline of Hindu history is so long—and so much material was destroyed during hundreds of years of Islamic invasion and Muslim rule, followed by colonialism—sometimes what is commonly understood as history is not what Hindus wrote. Often it is what their conquerors wrote.

There are two or three controversial pillars that Hindus need to address and, in my opinion, we should just face up to them. These are the history of invasions in India, specifically the nearly 1,000-year history of Islamic invasions in India, including the Mughal rule from 1526 to 1857; the history of caste discrimination in Hinduism; and, a more recent debate, the attitude towards homosexuality. The last one, gay rights, is actually not just an issue among conservative Hindus but among conservatives in all faiths, but my specific argument would be that Hindus have the strongest and most liberal position on gay rights, if only we would embrace it. The same logic can be extended to the treatment of transgender rights in India.

Let us take the issue of gay and transgender rights first. India still has a law that colonial British rulers made, Article 377, which treats homosexuality as an unnatural act punishable as a criminal offense. Why a modern, democratic nation—where a majority of the people profess to follow a sublimely liberal faith—still carries the colonial yoke of such an absurd and primitive law, no one knows. But there it is. It is even more ridiculous when one considers that Hindu mythology and cultural iconography is full of all kinds and forms of sexuality and gender bending.

Contemporary Hindu spiritual guru Sri Sri Ravi Shankar, whose Art of Living runs centers in more than 150 countries, has been vocal that homosexuality or transgender identity is neither seen as unnatural or a crime in Hinduism. He points out that, for instance, Lord Ayyappa, the Rig Veda deity who presides over the great Southern Indian shrine of Sabarimala (one of the most revered temples among Hindus) was born of Hari-Hara or Vishnu and Shiva, both male manifestations of the divine.

In her masterly work *Ardhanarishvara: The Androgyne*, the cultural critic Alka Pande says, "Homosexuality, gender-bending, cross-dressing and third gender expressions have always had a place in Indian art and culture."[1] She quotes the definitive example of the conceptual embrace of the idea in Hindu culture through the explanation of *Ardhanarishvara*, half man–half woman. Here is the mythological detail of the Ardhanarishvara as explained by Pande:

> The Ardhanarishvara has no desire. He is a composite—a single entity. It was the behest of Brahma's command that the Ardhanarishvara separated into the God and Goddess. Shiva divided himself and let his Shakti, power, be apprehended by both himself and Brahma. The great body of fire, of which erotic pleasures were the sparks, was dispersed. Duality was thus born. The great Goddess sent her glowing ardor, in the form of a woman, into the world of the gods. It was

thus from the origins of Ardhanarishvara's self-classification that burst forth the intricate idea of woman, sex and sensuality.[2]

There is even a god of the third gender, Mother Goddess Bahuchara, and therefore the idea of discrimination is something we have to shed now. There has been, without doubt, discrimination, especially against the third gender in India and a taboo about talking about gay relationships. But that is clearly ending in the country; after all it was a Hindu mother who placed the first ever matrimonial ad for a homosexual in India, and it is time that the law keeps up with what Hindus increasingly see as absolutely normal.

This is the newspaper advertisement that Padma Iyer, a so-called high-caste Brahmin, no less, placed in a newspaper for her gay rights activist son:

> Seeking 25–40, well placed, animal loving, vegetarian groom for my son 36, 5'11" who works with an NGO, caste no bar (though Iyer preferred).

It shows a dramatic mindset shift occurring in Hindu society and one that needs even better articulation and is no longer trapped in a colonial law. Now, in the two lines of advertisement above, notice that the mother, having thankfully given up gender and sexuality biases, would still prefer an Iyer candidate. Such is the subtle and sometimes vicious existence of the caste bias in India.

There have been endless debates on whether Gandhi and Vivekananda supported caste—even though in page after page of their writings, both men denounced untouchability and caste bias. Here is Gandhi's reply to Dalit leader (and eminent economist and author of India's constitution) B. R. Ambedkar in 1936: "Caste has nothing to do with religion. It is a custom whose origin I do not know and do not need to know for the satisfaction of my spiritual hunger. But I do know that it is harmful both to spiritual and national growth."[3]

In 1920, he wrote, "I consider untouchability to be a heinous crime against humanity. It is not a sign of self-restraint but an arrogant assumption of superiority."[4] Here he is again in 1927: "Whatever falls from truth should be rejected, no matter wherever it comes from, and therefore the burden lies on the shoulders of that person who upholds the practice which is inconsistent with truth, so that if a man wants to defend, for instance untouchability, he has to show that is it consistent with truth. Unless he shows that, all the authorities that he may cite in support of it are to me irrelevant."[5]

Vivekananda is equally vocal, "The Hindu faith has no hierarchy, no established authority. There is no persecution, no excommunication for dissenters within Hinduism. We must not forget that (the founder of Jainism) Mahavira and Buddha were born Hindus but chose to deviate from the authority of the Vedas. Modern degenerative influences have led to social evils like casteism and untouchability. I regard these tendencies as blots on the Hindu faith, which is essentially universal and all-encompassing."[6]

There has been continuous debate on whether people like Vivekananda and Gandhi, the men who envisioned the modern Indian nation, sufficiently condemned caste and whether they ought to have called for the complete destruction of Hinduism. One suspects that such debates will persist because certainly some of the argument is politically motivated on both sides.

In the meantime, all evidence suggests that caste structures are getting ever weaker in India. The primary attack on caste discrimination has come from twenty-five years of Indian economic liberalization—the free markets have weakened caste by beating social discrimination with economic mobility. There is data to prove this. Half of the Indian GDP (gross domestic product) comes from what is often called the Indian "informal sector." Credit Suisse says 90 percent of the Indian workforce is engaged in informal work, especially in rural areas.[7] The Organisation for Economic Co-operation and Development notes that 65 percent of manufacturing work is done by firms that have fewer than ten employees. Between 1999 and 2009, 75 percent of all new factories were built in rural India and 70 percent of new manufacturing jobs were created there.

So-called small-scale industries deliver 40 percent of Indian exports and 45 percent of industrial output. The informal sector has consistently grown faster than the formal sector for the last two decades and creates one million new jobs every year.[8]

Who are the beneficiaries of this sector? Let us look at the handloom industry, for instance. As Oxford economist Devaki Jain has pointed out, 75 percent of four million handloom workers are women. In handicrafts—where even in the middle of the global economic downturn of 2010–2011 exports grew—out of seven million workers, 48 percent are women. With growing demand in urban India for natural products, *khadi* (handspun fabric) now creates jobs for fourteen million people—a rise from 12.5 million between 2012–2013 and 2013–2014.[9]

That's not all. According to India's National Sample Survey data, 75 percent of informal sector firms are owned by scheduled castes, scheduled tribes, and other backward castes. These companies also deliver 71 percent of the manufacturing and 60 percent of the trading in the informal sector. Two-thirds of the handloom sector workers belong to underprivileged castes, and most of them work in rural areas. More than half of the workers in handicrafts are from minority or underprivileged groups.

There is also an illuminating report studying the impact of economic freedom on caste by a four-member team of researchers, comprising Devesh Kapur, the director for the Center for the Advanced Study of India at the University of Pennsylvania, Lant Prichett from the Kennedy School of Government at Harvard University, D. Shyam Babu of the Rajiv Gandhi Institute for Contemporary Studies, and Chandra Bhan Prasad, the foremost Indian scholar studying economics and caste. This study looked at all Dalit households (19,087) in two districts of Uttar Pradesh, Bilaria Ganj in the Azamgarh district in the east, and Khurja from the Bulandshahar district in the west to compare their lives before and after about twenty years of Indian economic liberalization from 1990 to 2008.[10]

What they found startled them. There had been a sea change in the ownership of consumer items such as bicycles, fans, TVs, and mobile phones. On an average, in both areas, around 50 percent more people were living in concrete homes in this period of economic growth, the number of TV set owners grew 33 percent, 45 percent more households had fans, and, of course, mobile phones were now in almost 35 percent of the households where previously there had been almost none. The following fact highlights just how impoverished the regions once were: for the first time, a quarter of households in both areas had chairs.

There was an even more intimate transformation. Most people rarely used toothpaste before liberalization, but a combined average of more than 65 percent use it now. Shampoo, another previously lacking ingredient in daily life, is currently used by nearly 70 percent.

What impact has this had on the centuries-long tradition of discrimination against those of lower castes, where upper-caste members have been forbidden to drink water from a glass touched by a Dalit or to eat from a plate used by a Dalit? The instances of upper-caste citizens eating and drinking at Dalit homes, once impossible to believe, rose more than 70 percent in the east and nearly 45 percent in the west. The practice that only Dalits clear up dead animals has almost disappeared.

Refusing to acknowledge caste in our private lives is a personal step we, each one of us, can adopt. As a country, we push good economics to bring income and livelihood to the most underprivileged part of our society. We should also break from caste discrimination, as has already been done in many parts of India. But beyond economics, it is pertinent also to recall the complexity of Indian caste history. One of the greatest warrior kings in the Hindu galaxy, the Maratha Shivaji from western India, was born into a lower caste. That has not stopped the faithful from worshipping him as one of the greatest Hindu heroes. As historian Shabnum Tejani has written, "Shivaji's broad appeal came not only from being acknowledged as a victorious warrior-king but also from the fact all classes and castes could lay claim to him . . . the strength of the Maratha polity could be attributed to Shivaji's Brahman (also spelt as Brahmin) mentor Ramdas. The wars against Muslim rule, therefore, could be read as having been fought with the intention to protect cows and Brahmans. . . . Or Shivaji's attempt to balance the power between

high and low castes allowed an interpretation of Maharashtra's historical and cultural traditions as emphasizing social harmony and a synthesis between local tradition and classical Hinduism."[11]

It might also be worth remembering that Jyotiba Phule, the father of
Indian social reforms and anti-caste fighter, was one of the greatest
champions of the legend of Shivaji. Forgotten also are the heroics of
Raja Sukhdeo (also known as Raja Suheldev), the lower-caste king
whose decimation in 1033 CE in the battle of Bahraich of an invading
army led by Salar Masud, a nephew of Sultan Mahmud Ghaznavi,
halted the Islamic invasion of India by nearly a century. So, while there
is no denying the long history of caste discrimination, it is impossible to
ignore the evidence of lower castes rising spectacularly to the defense
of Hinduism in history.

Now, to an equally conflict-ridden question: how do contemporary
Hindus to look at the history of Islam in India from the early invasions,
Mughal rule, and right up to having a Muslim president and vice presi-
dent in today's India?

There is an understanding among most Hindus that while there is
little doubt that Hindu civilization went through hundreds of years of
plunder, assault, destruction of holy places, and forced conversions by
Muslim invaders, it is also true that during parts of Mughal rule the
interaction between the two cultures—Islamic and Hindu (Persian and
Sanskrit)—brought about many collaborative treasures in everything
from literature, dance, music, food, to architecture.

Will Durant—celebrated historian, philosopher, and author of the
eleven-volume *Story of Civilization*, who was awarded the Pulitzer
Prize and the Presidential Medal of Freedom—encapsulated that story
of plunder in his famous line: "The Islamic conquest of India is probably the bloodiest story in history. It is a discouraging tale, for its evident moral is that civilization is a precious good, whose delicate complex of order and freedom, culture and peace, can at any moment be
overthrown by barbarians invading from without or multiplying within."[12] Let us take one more illuminating example. Harvard's Diana Eck,
whom we have referred to earlier as well, writes in her scholarly book

on Benaras about the number of times the city of Benaras, one of the holiest for the Hindus, faced plunder and destruction from Islamic invaders. "In 1206, with the establishment of the Delhi Sultanate, the entire Ganges valley came under Muslim domination. There were certainly high moments in these centuries, when Kashi recaptured something of its lost glory. There were times of ambitious temple construction and stimulating scholarly activity. But for the most part these were hard centuries. The religious life of the city was under almost constant threat. At least six times during these years the temples of Kashi were destroyed."[13]

This captures in a paragraph the Hindu perspective to Islamic rule even today—neither denying the moments that were amicable and symbiotic between Hinduism and Islam, nor hiding or covering the gruesome bloodshed. As Eck notes, during the reign of the Emperor Akbar several temples were protected and some built anew but his grandson Shah Jahan, the maker of the Taj Mahal, destroyed as many as seventy-six temples at Benaras alone, and Aurangzeb, the most fanatical of them all, did the maximum damage—"Some of the city's greatest temples, including Vishveshvara, Krittivasa and Bindu Madhava, were razed during the reign of Aurangzeb, and their sites were forever sealed from Hindu access by the construction of mosques. In his zeal for crushing Hindu idolatry, Aurangzeb even tried to rename the city 'Muhammadabad,'"[14] writes Eck.

How does an ordinary Hindu today consider this beyond political debate? Simply by accepting and recognizing the history and violence in it, and also by embracing the instances of Akbar or Dara Shukoh, who attempted to bridge the gap between the faiths by getting the *Upanishads* translated to Persian, believing that there was, in reality, no real difference except in terminology between the Vedic teachings and the *Quran*. Also consider Wajid Ali Shah, the last Nawab of Awadh (modern-day Lucknow in north India), who is responsible for the revival of the Indian classical dance Kathak and wrote plays on the love between the god Krishna and his consort Radha.

The modern Hindu is going through a period of assessment and contemplation with regard to history. In embracing both the dark and illuminating bits, one hopes to move from truth to reconciliation.

9

HOW DOES HINDUISM FIT INTO THE INTERNET AGE?

If artificial intelligence is the future, and machines will soon be smarter than human beings, then what in all this happens to our quest for God?

We are consistently told that our extensive use of technology and the Internet is changing the way our brains work. It might be shortening our attention spans, causing a deeper sense of isolation, and even pushing some towards suicide. Our brains are getting rewired. Some scientists suggest that as a result of this rewiring, our ability to learn, deeply understand a subject or a topic, and focus and absorb deteriorates quite rapidly as we accustom our brains to short and rapidly changing bursts of stimuli which the Internet is so proficient at providing. The writer Nicholas Carr complained in *Atlantic* magazine in 2008, asking rhetorically, "Is Google making us stupid?" He wrote, "what the Net seems to be doing is chipping away my capacity for concentration and contemplation. My mind now expects to take in information the way the Net distributes it: in a swiftly moving stream of particles. Immersing myself in a book or a lengthy article used to be easy. My mind would get caught up in the narrative or the turns of the argument, and I'd spend hours strolling through long stretches of prose. Now my concentration often starts to drift after two or three pages. The deep reading that used to come naturally has become a struggle."[1]

Not giving up the fight, Carr went on to write a book called *The Shallows*, wherein he argued, "If, knowing what we know today about the brain's plasticity, you were to set out to invent a medium that would rewire our mental circuits as quickly and thoroughly as possible, you would probably end up designing something that looks and works a lot like the Internet."[2]

There are many of us—perhaps most of us—who have felt, at some point or the other, what Carr is talking about. Once we spoke about being constantly connected; now we talk about digital detox.

But, in the meantime, something else is happening. Technology is moving beyond the realm of just transforming our activities. It is starting to push us to reimagine how we contemplate, not just how we see things, but also how we perceive them.

For one, there is this sense of everything being connected to everything else to complete an unbroken, unbreakable chain or whole. At any given moment, whether you are renting a room on Airbnb, hiring a ride on BlaBlaCar, registering to eat a home-cooked meal at someone's house, or selling a secondhand camera or laptop through a mobile app, all that binds it together is trust. "The Future of the Sharing Economy Depends on Trust" says a *Forbes* magazine essay. Who was the man writing the article? Stephen Ufford, the founder and CEO of Trulioo, which specializes in providing ever-higher levels of verified identity for the new world of shared business to survive and thrive.

Trust of course is increasingly tougher to cultivate in a world with more walls going up and the ease of travel going down.

This new world is based on a growing customer base of millennials—people who are in their twenties and thirties today—but this generation of people, says Pew Research, doesn't really trust easily. Only 19 percent of millennials believe most people can be trusted, compared with 35 percent for an older generation.[3]

So, one of the biggest challenges for our technology-driven world is actually a very, very old question—who can you trust? And how do you build trust? It is a question we have been asking since cousins fought each other to death, and Arjun was troubled by the thought of massacring family members in the battle of Kurukshetra. It a question we have been asking since Cain fought Abel.

Building trust is also a question mark on another simultaneous technological advance—singularity. Singularity sees our world moving steadily in a direction where the difference between man and machine completely disappears. The human and the machine create a singular composite by means of genetic transformation, nanotechnology, and artificial intelligence. From this point onward, the collective machine intelligence will be greater than the collective human intelligence. The term "singularity" was coined by scientist and writer Vernor Vinge and made popular by futurist Ray Kurzweil.

The idea is that slowly, computational technology will reach a level where it will have the capacities of the human brain. This will surpass the boundaries of the famous Moore's Law (named after cofounder of Intel, Gordon E. Moore), which predicts that capacities of integrated circuits will grow exponentially but not indefinitely and infinitely. But Kurzweil says that a new paradigm will leapfrog the challenges of integrated circuits and keep the exponential growth of computational capacity. Among the things he believes could provide that impetus are "nanotubes and nanotube circuitry, molecular computing, self-assembly in nanotube circuits, biological systems emulating circuit assembly, computing with DNA, spintronics (computing with the spin of electrons), computing with light, and quantum computing."[4]

These theories are the bedrock of Kurzweil's famous 2005 book, *The Singularity is Near*. But, and this is the most interesting question, even Kurzweil accepts that there is "no objective test that can conclusively determine"[5] the presence of consciousness. It is something we would have to take for granted.

Anyone who reads the Vedanta—or a Vedantin, to use the common term for a student of the Vedanta—cannot but recognize these ideas. This idea of a common, integrated approach to intelligence is the very soul of the Vedanta.

This is also the source of its eternal relevance. If you simultaneously read the Vedanta and about scientific advances, you cannot help but come to the conclusion that the theories and ideas are similar. Science is perhaps moving ever closer to the Vedanta idea of the universe.

The idea that the intelligence of the universe is one, and that we have only touched the tip of its individual manifestation, is not new to the Vedanta. Nor is the notion that without rising above our genetic selfishness, our Dawkinsian "selfish gene," we cannot build a new universe of cooperation and trust. *Aatma vikas*, the true revelation of the soul and the unity therein is, as the *Mundaka Upanishad* says, *sarva vidya pratistha*, or the basis of all sciences.

British evolutionary biologist Julian Huxley understood this. In his lecture "The Evolutionary Vision" he said, "Although it is to his mind that man owes both his present dominant position in evolution and any advances he may have made during his tenure of that position, he is still strangely ignorant, even superstitious about it. The exploration of the mind has barely begun. It must be one of the main tasks of the coming era, just as was the exploration of the world's surface a few centuries ago. Psychological exploration will doubtless reveal as many surprises as did geographical exploration and will make available to our descendents all kinds of new possibilities of fuller and richer being."[6]

If you think about it, what creates greater trust between people than anything else? Isn't it the understanding that there is, in reality, very little difference between them?

No matter what you call it, singularity or the trust economy, the basis of it all is the recognition of the oneness of the universe. It is this oneness of the consciousness that forms the foundation of our material search for oneness, whether it is through artificial intelligence or by building a sharing economy instead of one based on private ownership.

British astrophysicist Fred Hoyle recognized this. In his 1983 book, *The Intelligent Universe*, Hoyle says, "The picture of the origin of the universe, and of the formation of the galaxies and stars, as it has unfolded in astronomy, is curiously indefinite, like a landscape seen vaguely in a fog. This indefinite, unsatisfactory state of affairs contrasts with other parts of astronomy where the picture is bright and clear. A component has evidently been missing from cosmological studies. The origin of the universe, like the solution of the Rubik's Cube, requires an intelligence."[7]

When we think about singularity, it is important to remember Swami Vivekananda's words, "Science is nothing but the finding of unity. . . . Through multiplicity and duality, that ultimate unity is reached. . . . This is the goal of all science. All science is bound to come to this conclusion in the long run. Manifestation, and not creation, is the word of science today, and the Hindu is only glad that what he has been cherishing in his bosom for ages is going to be taught in more forcible language, and with further light from the latest conclusions of science."[8]

I am interested in exploring the nature of sanatana dharma in the Internet age because for too long, Hinduism has been correlated—with astonishing inaccuracy—with primitive and unscientific beliefs. In reality, of course, the more you read the Vedanta, the more you are convinced not only of the meeting point between technology and Hindu philosophy but also its future as an integrated whole.

If you think about it, it is the Vedanta that is seeking the same ends as the future of science; how do we arrive at unity? And when we do, where does our consciousness fit into this universe of technological commonality? There is an understanding that without comprehending the unity of the consciousness, the unity of intelligence is incomplete and redundant. For singularity to be achieved with harmony, the unity of the consciousness must be the platform on which the unity of intelligence stands.

In this, two arguments made by Fred Hoyle are strikingly relevant. First, again in *The Intelligent Universe*, he says, "It is a strange aspect of science that until now it has kept consciousness firmly out of any discussions of the material world. Yet it is with our consciousness that we think and make observations, and it seems surprising that there should be no interaction between the world of the mind and matter. Instead of picturing ourselves as external observers, quantum mechanics seems to imply that we cannot separate ourselves from the events that we are observing, sometimes to the extent of actually determining what takes place."[9]

Think about this: what are we really trying to achieve, for instance, through singularity? We are trying to reveal that the universe—as the Vedanta upholds and quantum theory is telling us with much greater, richer detail—is a union of intelligence that governs every activity in it that can be achieved.

We are building a network that recognizes that we are manifestations of the same whole, and therefore, have ever-rising levels of trust for deeper, richer, more intimate, and more sustainable relationships that do not seek ownership but only lasting affection. The recognition that our lives and each of our interactions are in essence transient, and yet the way to embrace them is by being completely trusting and totally present in that moment, is the only way to achieve harmony with the universe.

What is or where is God in all this then?

Fred Hoyle asks a very relevant question. "So starting from astronomy and biology with a little physics, we have arrived at religion. What happens if the situation is inverted, and we look at science from the religious point of view? How do the two approaches match up? The answer to this question turns on the form of theology. In contemporary Western teachings, the points of contact are few, essentially because god is placed outside the universe and in control of it. By contrast, in many other religions past and present [like the Vedanta], deities lie very much within the universe."[10] This placing of God "within the universe" is what makes Hinduism even more relevant in the Internet age.

If you think this view is not mainstream or is too esoteric, then you are wrong. In 2014, eighty scientists—including professors from Harvard, Cambridge, Cornell, and Princeton—from around the world, including one Nobel Prize winner, called for more research into the study of consciousness.

And if that doesn't convince you, there's even an app called "Collective Consciousness" that explores just this—our innate connections with each other. It explores how our minds are connected to our physical reality, which the PEAR (Princeton Engineering Anomalies Research) lab and the Institute of Noetic Sciences are also studying. Just so that you don't think that all this is too boring, the team that built it, apart from Silicon Valley and Princeton techies, also includes a man who was the tech go-to-guy of Lady Gaga.

As I came to the end of this book, I read an essay by historian Yuval Noah Harari on big data. Harari rose to fame with his enlightening book *Sapiens*, a sprawling history of the species. In a piece published in the *Financial Times*, he argued that we live in a world where data analytics is the new unquestionable authority—quite like the way, in fact, we once thought about God. We are shifting the decision-making power that makes us human to big data, allowing it to influence our choices about everything from what books and clothes we buy to whom we date. "[E]ven if Dataism is wrong about life, it may still conquer the world. Many previous creeds gained enormous popularity and power despite their factual mistakes. If Christianity and communism could do it, why not Dataism? Dataism has especially good prospects, because it is currently spreading across all scientific disciplines. A unified scientific paradigm may easily become an unassailable dogma. If you don't like this, and you want to stay beyond the reach of the algorithms, there is probably just one piece of advice to give you, the oldest in the book: know thyself. In the end, it's a simple empirical question. As long as you have greater insight and self-knowledge than the algorithms, your choices will still be superior and you will keep at least some authority in your hands. If the algorithms nevertheless seem poised to take over, it is mainly because most human beings hardly know themselves at all," wrote Harari.[11]

As a Hindu, two things immediately occurred to me when I read this—one, Harari is making the Dawkins mistake. The examples of authority he provides are Christianity and Communism—both of which, for the most part, base their tenets on one truth and one book. That's not how a Hindu looks at authority.

Second, his advice—know thyself—*is* the main mantra, the founding principle of Hinduism. If there is one underlying principle of Hindu thought it is that there is no answer but to know yourself; only by knowing yourself is the finding of any answers possible.

It seems Hinduism might have some relevance in the world of Data-ism after all.

10

A START-UP FOR THE SOUL

Why Reexamine the Hindu Way?

One of the last things I read as I finished this book was American writer Alan Watts's *The Book: On the Taboo Against Knowing Who You Are*. His writing draws from a variety of Eastern sources of engaging with the divine, from Hinduism to Buddhism and Jainism, but this particular book is extremely dedicated to applying the Vedanta in the world that the writer saw around him.

In it, Watts takes the very basic idea of the Vedanta and constructs a way of life that could be led on that basis. What is that idea? That idea is that there is no difference between you, or me, and the rest of the world that we see around us. At the very fundamental level there is unity, not difference.

Everything that we do ought to raise us to a greater awareness of this unity. As Seamus Heaney wrote,

> Here on earth my labours were
> The stepping stones to upper air.
> Lives that suffer and come right
> Are backlit by immortal light. [1]

But almost everything we do actually does not.

I wrote this book because I have lived my entire adult life in India, where the question of faith seems to consistently creep into our public and private existence. It has been deeply present in our political lives and certainly unavoidable in our social lives. But I could not, in my readings, find a contemporary record of going through the many pulls and pressures, the everyday friction of considering God.

Our education system—though it is called a system, it is perhaps better described as our education anarchy—certainly seems inadequate to deal with a question that often arises at the most inopportune moments.

There were gods and goddesses at home and prayers and hymns at school. The festivals and holidays were full of them. Names of the Almighty were whispered when one was unwell, was being tucked into bed, and when people arrived or left home—a small prayer to wish them safe travel. There was no place where a bit of religion did not turn up. When one was thrilled or when something was achieved, one was told to give thanks in His name. *"Jao thakur ke pronam kore esho"* (go say a prayer of thanks to God), my mother would say. One would dutifully take off the rubber slippers one wore at home, scrape the feet on the coir mat outside the little puja *ghar* at one corner of the house, and say a little prayer. The words of that prayer are what I mutter even today, *"Thakur, bhakti dao, subuddhi dao / Tomate moti dao, gyan dao."* God, please give me devotion, (good) intelligence / Set my mind on you, grant me wisdom.

In this prayer, I later realized, lay hidden the deepest desires and anxieties of my parents and also their most overwhelming humility and simplicity, for what were they teaching me to ask for? This was not a prayer that could be found in any book or sermon or hymn. This was the invention of my parents. This came straight from the most reticent recesses of their simple hearts.

It took me years to understand this, but the dominant theme in the life of my parents was fear. They were children of the Partition. Their parents had left what is now Bangladesh and everything they owned there, fleeing to India. The stories they heard as children were, in equal measure, redolent of a fertile past and merciless slaughter.

My parents had the instinct of loss hardwired in them. They did not remember the sights, nor recall the smells, but they had been told stories. Those stories told them that the world was not to be trusted and one never entirely lets the guard down.

It also taught them another thing. My grandmother used to tell me, "All you really have lies inside your head." On summer afternoons when I lay in bed listening to her stories from her village in Bangladesh, about the big fishes in the ponds, the meals cooked every day to feed at least one hundred people and endless rice fields wherever you looked, I wondered what that meant. How can all that we have be in our heads? Did I not have the house we lived in? The clothes? What about my mother's brass utensils? My father's old wrist watch? Our new clothes bought every Durga Puja?

One day, while saying the little prayer my parents taught to me, I finally understood what my grandmother meant. It was all hidden in that prayer. What did my parents ask me to pray for? Devotion, intelligence, and also wisdom. Curiously, for people who had only heard stories all their lives from their parents about how much they had lost during Partition, their plea was not for material well-being, nor for a roof over their head or food to eat, but for a sound mind. All you have, they understood, lies in your head.

But in the years when I began to, on rote, repeat this prayer, no one explained to me what it really meant and why it was of use to me. No one told me what do to with this thing called God. What did we have to do with religion? What could we? We stumbled upon God, as we had stumbled upon so many other things. Where was the book or the person who would tell us, as Alan Watts realized, that "true humor is laughter at oneself, true humanity is knowledge of oneself."[2] But where was that self whose knowledge we needed to gain? Who would or could guide us to that soul? We had no answers.

In his book, Alan Watts addresses what he sees as the fundamental disconnect that many Christians feel from the idea of God as explained by that faith, and he explains that it has to do with the monochromatic image of God as the father figure.

"Our Father, who art in heaven"—it all begins from that image, says Watts.[3] This reflects in the lives of ordinary people too, he says, where children see the male parent as someone who goes away each day to earn money that is then spent at home.

"The younger members of our society have for some time been in growing rebellion against paternal authority and the paternal state. For one reason, the home in an industrial society is chiefly a dormitory, and the father does not work there, with the result that wife and children have no part in his vocation. He is just a character who brings in money, and after working hours he is supposed to forget about his job and have fun," wrote Watts. "All this is further aggravated by the fact that parents no longer educate their own children. Thus the child does not grow up with understanding of or enthusiasm for his father's work."[4]

When I read this, I wondered two things. First, it dawned on me that I had had no insight or education into the profession that my father spent all his life involved in—that of a railway civil engineer. I was proud that he had helped build India's first metro or tube railway networks in two cities—Calcutta and Delhi—but I knew nothing else about his work. What did he do every day when he went to work? What were his dreams and aspirations? The truth is I did not know, and even today, do not know as much as I should. What did this lack of knowledge really mean? It meant that, for me, my father and my mother remained access points to material and emotional succor. I knew little about them, and what I did seemed disturbingly transactional. This also made me think of my understanding of God and myself. Who was I a supplicant to? What kind of transactions was I trying to effect with God? Why was I encouraged, like so many millions of my coreligionists, to quickly barter some blessings from God every time there was trouble?

How many Hindus really know why they pray? What do the mantras mean, and why do they mouth them? No one taught us to understand that the act of prayer is really inward, not outward, and that in the act of seeking, all you can ever hope to receive is the understanding of that which lies within you.

We grow up believing that to pray is to reach out to the external, that which lies outside of us. All the while, in reality, we are seeking something that lies within us. Our relationship with God, we are led to believe when we grow older, is irrational hocus pocus. It is not just embarrassingly naïve but condemnably stupid to be discussing matters like faith. The opiate of the masses is not for us, for we are, presumably, not the masses.

Our ideologies are external, as also our notions of home. The first buds of civilization are often dismissed as maudlin, regressively sentimental, and precociously brushed away as "conditioning."

But the idea of God, like the idea of home, never quite goes away. Especially if you have grown up with that idea popping up everywhere, from calendar art to holiday feasts. This is why understanding how you or I feel about it, how we negotiate it, how we address it, and what it means to us is so important.

Cultural historian Peter Gay in his ambitious study of modernism described it as "far easier to exemplify than describe."[5] The reason why we need or seek this ephemeral idea called God is also that—far easier to exemplify than describe. The more I thought about this, the more I understood that this journey of understanding God, which is also one's real self, opens to us our most complicated needs. For instance, our need to be vulnerable.

What is prayer if not a lesson in the profound power of vulnerability? Prayer teaches us that to be vulnerable is to be human, even alive.

But the idea that one prays for external sustenance is not the basis of the sanatana dharma. Wonderfully, if you contemplate this, Hinduism teaches that your prayers are truly directed, in a sense, to yourself. You are praying to yourself. That kind of blows your mind to begin with, and then there is a trickle of recognition that this is curiously liberating. It brings a new perspective to what has been thought of as primitive. You start to recognize that the power of prayer, for instance, is a process of addressing long-neglected parts of your psyche. It is the process of truth telling, to yourself. I was once asked if Hinduism had its own version of the confessional chamber, where a priest calmly listens to your admission of guilt and frailty. I pondered that and came to the conclusion that sanatana dharma did in fact have a sense of disgorging the truths from the soul, with one difference—the confession here is to oneself. The speaker and the listener is you.

So, I feel that understanding how we relate to God is far from futile. Understanding how you relate to the idea which you turn to—sometimes perhaps almost embarrassingly in your most helpless moments—can hardly be useless. In fact, it is entirely seminal in our individual journeys. It is only through this travel that we come to appreciate that there isn't one individual journey; it is the manifestation of the larger path the universe takes. Alan Watts described the Vedanta's view on this as the third way.

Apart from both the "sacred individual—the unique personal ego, separate from both nature and God"[6] (essentially the extreme capitalist view of man) and (the Communist view) of man as "the cog in the industrial-collectivist machine, or the mere 'hand'"[7] (as the factory worker is often called), the third way is what the Vedanta prescribes and Watts describes as, the human being "seen . . . as one particular focal point at which the whole universe expresses itself—as an incarnation of the self, of the godhead, or whatever one may choose to call it."[8]

The realization of this is the step-by-step process of understanding the idea of God and the process of prayer. Why do we fail to appreciate this? Perhaps it is because we have been led to believe that searching for anything that even remotely talks about God is somehow old-fashioned, if not barbaric.

The beauty of Hinduism is that sanatana dharma and its principles are so fundamentally universal, and so personal, that the question of them being dated does not arise. How can your search for yourself become regressive?

Mahatma Gandhi understood this and spent his life trying to explain it. In 1927, responding to a question, he said, "I accept no authority or any *shashtra* (scriptural text) as an infallible guide. I reject the claim that we should accept the whole if we accept a part." He was then asked, "Then would you accept what is convenient and reject what is inconvenient?"

"That's a good question," Gandhi replied. "Hinduism is not a codified religion. In Hinduism we have got this remarkable foot rule to measure every shashtra and every rule of conduct, and that is truth. Let us not deceive ourselves into the belief that everything that is written in Sanskrit and printed in shashtras has any binding effect upon us. That which is opposed to the maxims of morality, that which is opposed to trained reason, cannot be claimed as shashtra no matter how ancient it may be."[9]

But what is this truth? Where does it come from? Who builds or creates these "maxims of morality"? And "trained reason" according to whom?

In 1940, Gandhi was even more emphatic about where his morality and trained reason came from, "My reason follows my heart. Without the latter, it would go astray. Faith is the function of the heart. It must be reinforced by reason. The two are not antagonistic as some think. The more intense one's faith is, the more it whets one's reason. I have not put my reason in cold storage. When faith becomes blind, it dies."[10]

These are critical questions. As resonant as they were when Gandhi answered them, they are perhaps even more so today as modernity asks that we bare ever more intimate parts of ourselves, dismantling and disintegrating what feels like our very selves. The Church faces one of the most turbulent times in its history, Islam is ravaged by bloodshed, and even Buddhism in Myanmar, Sri Lanka, and some parts of China is witnessing aggressive streaks. We are told that Hinduism in India is turning ever more hardline. It is, therefore, more critical than ever to define not just what being Hindu means but also what it does not mean; that to be Hindu is to be plural is not enough. We must aggressively proclaim that to be Hindu is to shun bigotry, to accept diversity, to embrace differences, to respect gender rights, and to actively adopt new technologies and sciences.

The irreverent is a valuable part of the Hindu worldview but not the irrational.

To debate what constitutes a "good Hindu" is futile and dangerously veers towards the old "good Muslim/bad Muslim" trap. It is infinitely better to chart out acceptable ideologies in our times. For instance, discrimination on the basis of birth is unacceptable, no matter which ritual, faith, or priest says so.

Finally, it is the ethics of the ideology and not the subjective ethics of the applicant that ought to determine the trajectory of a religion. Therefore, the idea worth promoting is that any Hindu seeking to understand his faith ought to turn to its core, its philosophies, and not its penances. It is on the generosity of Hinduism that a true Hindu identity can be built.

It is, in short, tougher than ever perhaps to be God, but only if you see God as a distant, mythical entity. Otherwise, you would have to argue that it has never been tougher to be you, wouldn't you?

In the age of start-ups, wherein every aspect of human life is, once again, being reimagined, and we are being told that everything will be disrupted, there is now an urgent need to build a new kind of start-up.

Why do we need such a start-up? What are we trying to disrupt? What, to be honest, ought to be disrupted? Maybe our sense of self? It is worth thinking about, is it not, where we draw our sense of self from? And how can we renegotiate the lines that give us an identity?

The idea that material possessions—this house, this car, that dress, and that piece of stone—will not do is so overstated that one is afraid that it has lost meaning. Even the adamantine refusal of objectification has, sadly, itself become objectified.

Can we then consider not so much the problem but the solution? How do we disrupt what we think about our very souls? What makes it soulful? In our pursuit of happiness, how do we embrace the pensive?

A start-up that will enable us to see that the pursuit of happiness is always bound to fail if there is a pursuit. Happiness, like God-realization, comes from within, but as always, we have externalized something to be pursued. But what if a new start-up, a new disruptive way of thinking about our lives, could tell us that anything we imagine to be outside us that we need to find, hunt down, conquer, possess, own, capture, put behind lock and key, well, that thing then, is unlikely to make us happy?

It is like that image so many of us were so enamored with when we were young—that of a naked Howard Roark standing on a cliff and laughing, the ultimate Ayn Rand vision presented in *The Fountainhead* of a world and nature, conquered by the sheer will of man.

Why am I quoting Ayn Rand, of all people? Because simplistic as she is—and sometimes even discredited in many parts of the world, certainly in mine—Rand was vitally part of a growing-up experience, a lesson in unfettered raw individualism that seemed so wild, passionate, and attractive at one point. For me, this was no doubt because I grew up in a Communist-ruled state in India. Communists controlled the eastern Indian state of Bengal for more than thirty years, and during this time, they took a prosperous, industrial state and turned it into one of the most impoverished, derelict, and violent in the country. Two generations of Bengalis fled from jobless, despairing Calcutta, slowly, somnolently falling to pieces. In such an environment, Rand made sense.

When I look at politics around the world today, and the most unbridled passions against, and even for, globalization, I am constantly reminded of the shadowless philosophy of Ayn Rand. Such uncompromising certitude, I have grown to believe, hides either insecurity or ignorance—sometimes both. My personal journey with my faith, with Hindu philosophy has helped me look at the world with new eyes, with a confidence that needs neither bluster nor inexactitude. And it is to explain how different and nuanced my ideas of life have become through Hinduism that I mention Rand and her merciless heroes at this point.

Read the following paragraphs carefully. Most likely you have read them before. But perhaps I could convince you to relook at them. Try and reanalyze with me their message and its worldview.

> Howard Roark laughed. He stood naked at the edge of a cliff. . . .
> The lake below was only a thin steel ring that cut the rocks in half.
> The rocks went on into the depth, unchanged. They began and ended in the sky. So that the world seemed suspended in space, an

island floating on nothing, anchored to the feet of the man on the cliff. . . . His face was like a law of nature—a thing one could not question, alter or implore. It had high cheekbones over gaunt, hollow cheeks; gray eyes, cold and steady; a contemptuous mouth, shut tight, the mouth. . . . He looked at the granite. These rocks, he thought, are here for me; waiting for the drill, the dynamite and my voice; waiting to be split, ripped, pounded, reborn; waiting for the shape my hands will give them.

It is a tantalizingly addictive image, isn't it? There is something about the idea of man being in supreme control of his will. But this kind of control is the antithesis of the supreme divine power of man that Vivek-ananda spoke about. Why?

Read the words carefully. Through it all flows the notion of the supremacy of man over all he surveys, the sense that it all exists to be conquered by man, while man stands aloof and arrogant from it all, confident of his hegemony, his ultimate victory in a conflict to dominate and subjugate all that he surveys. "So that the world seemed suspended in space, an island floating on nothing, anchored to the feet of the man on the cliff."

I used to love this opening mise-en-scène; this sense of haughty grandeur, this confidence that finally man wins. But at some point, as I started reading the Vedanta, I began to question—wins against what? What is man's victory over? What are we conquering? And to what end? Where is all our incessant conquest leading us? Is it, as Alan Watts remarked scornfully, a bit like what the Red Queen said?

Here's what happens in Lewis Carroll's *Through the Looking Glass*, the follow-up adventures of Alice after Wonderland:

"Well, in our country," said Alice, still panting a little, "you'd general-ly get to somewhere else—if you run very fast for a long time, as we've been doing."

"A slow sort of country!" said the Queen. "Now, here, you see, it takes all the running you can do, to keep in the same place. If you want to get somewhere else, you must run at least twice as fast as that!"[11]

In science fiction, this is known as the predestination paradox—caught in an endless loop between two incidents of time travel, you continue to vacillate between them, seemingly without possibility of escape.

Is our endless conquest a bit like that? Does it seem that we need to grow more, dig further and deeper, and exploit more while taking increasingly dangerous risks, just to stay in the same place and maintain the equilibrium of power in the world?

Unsurprisingly, the concept of the Red Queen's race has been used by at least one *Financial Times* columnist at the height of the economic downturn in 2010. The reference was to a speech by Andrew Haldane, chief economist and executive director of monetary analysis and statistics at the Bank of England, who wailed about a progressive rise in banking risk and at the same time, the governmental safety net getting deeper and wider. The *FT* columnist pointed out that this was a Red Queen's race with "the system running to stand still with governments racing to make finance safer and bankers creating more risk." Our world teaches us to run swiftly just to remain in the same place but fails to ask: do we really want to be in that place?

Such questions are not encouraged, are they? They are dismissed as escapist, irrelevant, impractical and even "loser-like." The almost colonial urge to subjugate or the Stalinist desire to force fit—those are our only options. In this, Rand has chosen her side.

Every description that Rand lined up for her hero was drained of what she saw as weak-kneed sentimentality. Roark is gaunt-cheeked, his eyes are cold and his mouth and veneer contemptuous. One sees what Rand was aiming at. A refugee from the excesses of Communism, she was painting the heroic individual against the tyranny of the masses, the superego versus the cog in the wheel; and in each, the superego wins.

But the world of the Vedantin recognizes the futility of both these approaches. And it is because these are the choices that the world mostly throws at us that we need a sense of our relationship with ourselves, with a mystery that goes deep into our subconscious. Ours is a world that serves sermons in playbooks for children and in self-help books for adults. The book we need though ought to do neither. It merely needs to push us to use that sense of rational morality that Gandhi preached, of which he said,

> I have no hesitation in rejecting scriptural authority of a doubtful character. . . . Indeed I would reject all scriptural authority if it is in conflict with sober reason or the dictates of the heart. Authority sustains and ennobles the weak when it is the hand-work of reason, but it degrades them when it supplants reason sanctified by the still small voice within.[12]

We need a new kind of start-up that helps us answer the questions within because no matter how many questions we address without, unless the ones within are answered, there cannot be peace. These answers do not need to be discovered. That is perhaps the happiest situation. We already know that they exist. We know where to find them, and we know that they lie in the collective consciousness of humankind. What we have not yet managed is a seamless, everyday way for everyone to access the answers, or even start on the process of accessing the answers.

How do you begin? By understanding that if you are going to stand naked on a cliff, enjoy the view and remember that it is all part of you.

NOTES

INTRODUCTION

1. Diana L. Eck, *Banaras: City of Light* (New Delhi: Penguin India, 1992), 3.

2. Eck, *Banaras*, 4.

3. Abhipsha Mahapatro, "Tulsi Gabbard Slams Reza Aslan, CNN Over Portrayal of Hinduism," *The Quint*, March 7, 2017, https://www.thequint.com/world/2017/03/08/tulsi-gabbard-slams-reza-aslan-cnn-believer-over-portrayal-of-hinduism.

4. Tulsi Gabbard, Twitter, March 7, 2017, https://twitter.com/TulsiGabbard/status/839211452904976384.

5. Gabbard, Twitter.

6. Vamsee Juluri, "CNN's 'Believer' Is Reckless, Racist and Dangerously Anti-Immigrant," *Huffington Post*, March 5, 2017.

7. Hindu American Foundation, "HAF Presents Community Concerns about 'Believer' to Show Host Reza Aslan, https://www.hafsite.org/haf-presents-community-concerns-about-believer-show-host-reza-aslan, March 5, 2017.

8. Juluri, "CNN's 'Believer' Is Reckless, Racist and Dangerously Anti-Immigrant."

9. Swami Vivekananda, *The Complete Works of Swami Vivekananda*, vol. 1 (Mayavati: Advaita Ashram, 2007), 3.

10. Rick Briggs, "Knowledge Representation in Sanskrit and Artificial Intelligence," *Artificial Intelligence Magazine* 6, no. 1 (1985).

11. Christopher Isherwood, "What Is Vedanta? An Introduction," in *Living Wisdom: Vedanta in a World Community,* ed. Pravrajika Vrajaprana (Chennai: Sri Ramakrishna Math, 1995), 13.

12. Nathuram Godse, *Why I Assassinated Mahatma Gandhi* (Delhi: Farsight Publishers, 2014), 47.

13. "Begin at the End: Introduction to Indian Philosophy," podcast, September 19, 2015, *History of Philosophy without Any Gaps*, https://historyofphilosophy.net/india-introduction.

1. HOW TO WRITE ABOUT HINDUS

1. Ananda K. Coomaraswamy, *The Dance of Shiva* (New Delhi: Munshiram Manoharlal Publishers, 2012).

2. D. R. Bhandarkar, *Lectures on the Ancient History of India* (New Delhi: Rupa Publications, 2013).

3. Caldwell was a Christian missionary and linguist in the second half of the nineteenth century.

4. Bhandarkar, *Lectures on the Ancient History of India.*

5. R. C. Majumdar, *The Vedic Age: The History and Culture of the Indian People*, vol. 1 (Mumbai: Bharatiya Vidya Bhawan, 1951), 27.

6. R. C. Majumdar, *The Vedic Age*, 27.

7. Subrata Dasgupta, *Awakening: The Story of the Bengal Renaissance* (New Delhi: Random House India, 2011), 38–39.

8. Binyavanga Wainaina, "How To Write About Africa," *Granta* 92 (January 19, 2006), http://granta.com/how-to-write-about-africa/.

2. WHO IS A HINDU?

1. James Mill, *History of British India* (London: Baldwin, Cradock and Joy, 1817).

2. John Stuart Mill, *On Liberty* (London: J. W. Parker and Son, 1859).

3. James Mill, *History of British India.*

4. James Mill, *History of British India*, 12.

5. Thomas R. Trautmann, *Aryans and British India* (Oakland: University of California Press, 1997), 117.

6. Diana L. Eck, *India: A Sacred Geography* (New York City: Harmony Books, 2012), 47.

7. T. N. Madan, et al., "Hinduism: An Introductory Essay," in *The Hinduism Omnibus* (New Delhi: Oxford University Press India, 2003), 12.

8. Blake Morrison, "Today's Past Master," *The Independent*, April 8, 1995.

9. Simon Schama, *Landscape and Memory* (London: Fontana Press, 1996), 9.

10. Radhakumud Mookerji, *Nationalism in Hindu Culture* (London: Theosophical Publishing House, 1921), 52.

11. A. K. Mazumdar, *The Hindu History* (Delhi: Rupa Publications, 2008), 39.

12. Eck, *India: A Sacred Geography*, 53.

13. Eck, *India: A Sacred Geography*, 55.

14. Swami Vivekananda, "The Future of India," Madras (Chennai), February 1897, in *Lectures from Colombo to Almora* (Belur Math: Advaita Ashrama, 2005), 215.

15. Vivekananda, *Lectures from Colombo to Almora*, 215.

16. R. C. Majumdar, ed., "Introduction," *The Vedic Age: The History and Culture of the Indian People* (New Delhi: Bharatiya Vidya Bhawan Educational Trust, G. Allen & Unwin, 1951).

17. Dilip K. Chakrabarti, "Power, Politics and Ariya Mayai," in *Nation First: Essays in the Politics of Ancient Indian Studies* (New Delhi: Aryan Books International, 2014), 116–117.

18. Kumar Chellappan, "New Research Debunks Aryan Invasion Theory," *DNA India* (December 10, 2011), http://www.dnaindia.com/india/report-new-research-debunks-aryan-invasion-theory-1623744.

19. Chellappan, "New Research Debunks Aryan Invasion Theory."

20. Sanghamitra Sengupta, et al., "Polarity and Temporality of High-Resoultion Y-Chromosome Distributions in India Indentify Both Indigenous and Exogenous Expansions and Reveal Minor Genetic Influence of Central Asian Pastoralists," *American Journal of Human Genetics* (February 2006).

21. Chakrabarti, *Nation First: Essays*, 116–117.

22. Chakrabarti, *Nation First: Essays*, 116–117.

23. Michel Danino, *Indian Culture and India's Future* (New Delhi: DK Printworld, 2011), 17.

24. Sanjeev Sanyal, *Land of the Seven Rivers* (New Delhi: Penguin India, 2012), 29–33.

25. "Six Mahavakyas," *The Hindu Universe*, http://www.hindunet.org/scriptures/mahavakyas/index.htm, and "Awakening of Intelligence," part 2, New York 197, *Jiddu-Kirshnamurti*, http://www.jiddu-krishnamurti.net/en/awakening-of-intelligence/1969-07-26-jiddu-krishnamurti-awakening-of-intelligence-four-mahavakyas-from-the-upanishads.

26. Shri Ramana Maharshi and Arthur Osborne, *The Teachings of Ramana Maharshi* (London: Rider Books, 2014), 7.

27. Sister Nivedita, *Footfalls of Indian History* (Belur Math: Advaita Ashrama, 2014), 164.

28. Vamsee Juluri, *Rearming Hinduism* (New Delhi: Westland Books, 2014), 5.

3. WHAT MAKES YOU A HINDU?

1. R. C. Majumdar, *The Vedic Age: The History and Culture of the Indian People*, vol. 1 (Mumbai: Bharatiya Vidya Bhawan, 1951), 38.

2. Lakshmidhar Mishra, *Human Bondage: Tracing its Roots in India* (New Delhi: Sage Publications India, 2011), 253.

3. David Frawley, *Hinduism: The Eternal Tradition* (New Delhi: Voice of India, 1995), 9.

4. Amaresh Datta, ed., *Encyclopaedia of Indian Literature*, vol. 2 (New Delhi: Sahitya Akademi, 2005), 150.

5. Kenan Malik, *The Quest for a Moral Compass: A Global History of Ethics* (New Delhi: Atlantic Books, 2014), 81.

6. Malik, *The Quest for a Moral Compass*, 81.

7. Sampooran Singh and Kanwaljit Kaur, *Symbiosis of Science and Spirituality: Generation of Innovation In Science for Human Survival* (New Delhi: Kalpaz Publications, 2006), 235.

8. Ken Wilber, ed., *Quantum Questions: Mystical Writings of the World's Greatest Physicists* (Boston: Shambhala Publications, 2001), 98.

9. Walter Moore, *Schrödinger: Life and Thought* (Cambridge: Cambridge University Press, 1989), 173.

10. Fritjof Capra, *The Tao of Physics (Flamingo)*, 2nd ed. (London: HarperCollins, 1983).

11. Capra, *The Tao of Physics*, 100.

12. Capra, *The Tao of Physics*, 141.

13. Capra, *The Tao of Physics*, 141.

14. *Mandukya Upanishad*, chapter 11, verse 2.29.

15. Alfred I. Tauber, ed., *Science and the Quest for Reality* (London: Macmillan, 1997), 128.

16. Interview with Ankur Barua.

17. Wilber, *Quantum Questions*, 5.

18. Wilber, *Quantum Questions*, 7.

19. Wilber, *Quantum Questions*, 8.

20. Wilber, *Quantum Questions*, 8.

21. Wilber, *Quantum Questions*, 8.

22. Wilber, *Quantum Questions*, 8.

23. John Horgan, "World's Smartest Physicist Thinks Science Can't Crack Consciousness: String Theorist Edward Witten Ways Consciousness 'Will Remain a Mystery,'" *Scientific American* (August 18, 2016).

24. Michel Danino, *Indian Culture and India's Future* (New Delhi: DK Printworld, 2011), 133.

25. *The Gospel of Sri Ramakrishna* (Chennai: Sri Ramakrishna Math, 1997), 80.

26. *The Gospel of Sri Ramakrishna*, 80.

27. C. G. Jung, *The Undiscovered Self: The Dilemma of the Individual in Modern Society* (New York City: Penguin Books USA, 2006), 23.

28. Jung, *The Undiscovered Self*, 24.

29. Jung, *The Undiscovered Self*, 24.

30. Jung, *The Undiscovered Self*, 24.

31. Roberto Calasso, *Ardor* (London: Penguin Books UK, 2013), 27.

32. http://isha.sadhguru.org/blog/lifestyle/music/mystic-chants-nirvana-shatakam/Isha Foundation.

33. J. Moussaieff Masson, *The Oceanic Feeling: The Origins of Religious Sentiment in Ancient India* (Dordrecht: D. Reidel Publishing Company, 1980), 44.

34. Jessica Orwig, "Neil deGrasse Tyson's 'Most Astounding Fact About The Universe' Will Bring You To Tears," *Business Insider* (November 5, 2014).

35. Alan W. Watts, *The Wisdom of Insecurity* (New York City: Pantheon Books, 1951), 54.

36. *Bhagavad Gita*, chapter 9, verse 13.

4. WHO IS THE ONE TRUE GOD?

1. http://www.ramakrishna.org/activities/message/message10.htm.

2. Rajiv Malhotra, "Tolerance Isn't Good Enough: The Need for Mutual Respect In Interfaith Relations," *Huffington Post* (December 9, 2010).

3. Seamus Heaney, "Seamus Heaney: His 10 Best Poems" ("The Tollund Man in Springtime"), *The Telegraph* (March 17, 2015).

4. Seamus Heaney, "Seamus Heaney: His 10 Best Poems" ("Untitled"), *The Telegraph* (March 17, 2017).

5. Beth Wright, *A Study Companion to Introduction to World Religions* (Minneapolis: Fortress Press, 2013), 52.

6. Swami Vivekananda, *Vedanta: Voice of Freedom*, ed. Swami Chetanananda (Belur Math: Advaita Ashram, 1987), 57, 61.

7. Vivekananda, *Vedanta: Voice of Freedom*, 57, 61.

8. Swami Dayanand Saraswati, "Silence In Spite of Thoughts," http://www.discovervedanta.com.

9. http://spiritualityandpractice.com/book-reviews/excerpts/view/19808/in-pursuit-of-silence.

10. "I'm An Ordinary Man," *My Fair Lady* soundtrack, lyrics by Alan Jay Lerner, http://www.metrolyrics.com/im-an-ordinary-man-lyrics-my-fair-lady.html

11. David Bollier, "On the Need for Silence and Solitude," blog, http://bollier.org/need-silence-and-solitude (April 1, 2012).

12. Pico Iyer, "The Joy of Quiet," *New York Times* (December 29, 2011).

13. Iyer, "The Joy of Quiet."

14. Sherry Turkle, "Connected, But Alone?" TED (Technology, Entertainment, Design) Talk, https://www.ted.com/talks/sherry_turkle_alone_together (February 2012).

15. Judith Shulevitz, "The Lethality of Loneliness: We Now Know How It Can Ravage Your Body and Mind," *New Republic* (May 13, 2013).

16. Frieda Fromme-Reichmann, *Principles of Intensive Psychotherapy* (Chicago: University of Chicago Press, 1960).

17. Fromme-Reichmann, *Principles of Intensive Psychotherapy*.

18. Fromme-Reichmann, *Principles of Intensive Psychotherapy*.

19. Fromme-Reichmann, *Principles of Intensive Psychotherapy*.

20. Robert Fisk, "Who Is Bombing Who in the Middle East?" *The Independent* (May 5, 2015).

21. Haridas Bhattacharya, *The Cultural Heritage of India*, vol. 1 (Calcutta: Ramakrishna Mission Institute of Culture, 2001), 350.

22. Turkle, "Connected, But Alone?"

23. Turkle, "Connected, But Alone?"

24. King James Bible, Book of Genesis 1:1–31, accessed at https://www.kingjamesbibleonline.org/Genesis-Chapter-1.

25. A. A. Macdonell, trans., *The Creation in Rig Veda*, 10:129 (1922), accessed at http://www.creationmyths.org/rigveda-10-129-indian-creation/rigveda-10-129-indian-creation-5-macdonell-translation.htm.

26. Macdonell, *The Creation in Rig Veda*.

27. Alan Watts, *The Wisdom of Insecurity: A Message for an Age of Anxiety* (New York City: Vintage Books, 2011), 26.

28. Nirad C. Chaudhuri, et al., "Hinduism: A Religion to Live By," in *The Hinduism Omnibus* (New Delhi: Oxford University Press India, 2003), 10.

29. Chaudhuri, et al., *The Hinduism Omnibus*, 10.

30. Diana L. Eck, *Banaras: City of Light* (New Delhi: Penguin India, 1992), 20.

31. M. M. Gopinath Kaviraj, *Selected Writings of M. M. Gopinath Kaviraj*, 2nd ed. (Varanasi: Indica Books, 2006), 44–45.

32. http://www.jkrishnamurti.org/krishnamurti-teachings/view-daily-quote/20091118.php?t=Meditation.

33. Swami Vivekananda, *Lectures from Colombo to Almora* (Belur Math: Advaita Ashrama, 2005), 240.

34. Richard Feynman, *The Pleasure of Finding Things Out* (London: Penguin Books UK, 1999), 247–248.

35. Feynman, *The Pleasure of Finding Things Out*, 249.

36. Feynman, *The Pleasure of Finding Things Out*, 251–252.

37. Feynman, *The Pleasure of Finding Things Out*, 255.

38. Devdutt Pattanaik, "East vs. West: The Myths that Mystify," TED Talk (India, 2009).

39. David Frawley, foreword, in *The Word as Revelation: Names of Gods*, by Ram Swarup (New Delhi: Voice of India, 2001), 14.

5. IS GOD AFRAID OF SCIENCE?

1. Richard Dawkins, *The God Delusion* (London: Bantam Press, 2006), 53

2. Dawkins, *The God Delusion*, 53.

3. Dawkins, *The God Delusion*, 53.

4. Dawkins, *The God Delusion*, 295.

5. Alan Lightman, *The Accidental Universe: The World You Thought You Knew* (New York: Vintage, 2013), 50–51.

6. Lightman, *The Accidental Universe*, 50–51.

7. Swami Vivekananda, *Complete Works of Swami Vivekananda*, vol. 6 (Belur Math: Advaita Ashram, 2001), 1559.

8. Vivekananda, *Complete Works*, vol. 6, 367.

9. Vivekananda, *Complete Works*, vol. 6, 1559.

10. Vivekananda, *Vedanta: The Voice of Freedom*, ed. Swami Chetanananda (Belur Math: Advaita Ashram, 1987), 255.

11. C. Rajagopalachari, *Hinduism: Doctrine and Way of Life* (New Delhi: Bharatiya Vidya Bhavan, 1959), 62.

12. Rajagopalachari, *Hinduism: Doctrine and Way of Life*, 62.

13. Ann Louise Bardach, "How Yoga Won the West," *The New York Times* (October 1, 2011).

14. B. V. Subbarayappa, *India's Contribution to World Thought and Culture: India's Contributions to the History of Science* (Chennai: Vivekananda Kendra Prakashan Trust, 1970), 49.

15. Subbarayappa, *India's Contribution to World Thought and Culture*, 49–50.

16. Subbarayappa, *India's Contribution to World Thought and Culture*, 50.

17. Subbarayappa, *India's Contribution to World Thought and Culture*, 51.

18. Denise Cush, Catherine Robinson, and Michael York, eds., *Encyclopedia of Hinduism* (New York: Routledge, 2007), 313.

19. Kim Plofker, *Mathematics in India* (Princeton, NJ: Princeton University Press, 2008), reviewed by David Mumford, *AMS Mathematical Society* (March 2010).

20. Plofker, *Mathematics in India*, Mumford review.

21. Plofker, *Mathematics in India*, Mumford review.

22. Plofker, *Mathematics in India*, Mumford review.

23. Subbarayappa, *India's Contribution to World Thought and Culture*, 51.

24. Subbarayappa, *India's Contribution to World Thought and Culture*, 51.

25. Michel Danino, *Indian Culture and India's Future* (New Delhi: DK Printworld, 2011), 28, 29.

26. Sangeetha Menon, "Hinduism and Science," in *The Oxford Handbook of Religion and Science,* ed. Philip Clayton and Zachary Simpson (Oxford: Oxford University Press UK, 2006), 14.

27. Subbarayappa, *India's Contribution to World Thought and Culture*, 58.

28. Subbarayappa, *India's Contribution to World Thought and Culture*, 58.

29. Danino, *Indian Culture and India's Future*, 66.

30. KumKum Dasgupta, "India's Missing Girls: Fears Grow Over Rising Levels of Foeticide," *The Guardian* (April 9, 2014).

31. Calculations made using data from the National Crime Records Bureau.

32. Text of 2016 Ramon Magsaysay award winner Bezwada Wilson, https://counterview.org/2016/07/28/recognising-moral-energy-prodigious-skill-in-movement-to-eradicate-manual-scavenging-in-india.

33. *Madhusudana Sarasvati Bhagavad Gita*, Swami Gambhirananda, trans. (Mayavati: Advaita Ashram, 2007), 277-278.

34. K. D. Gangrade, *Moral Lessons from Gandhi's Autobiography and Other Essays* (New Delhi: Concept Publishing, 2004), 78.

6. HOW DO HINDU BOOKS PORTRAY GOD?

1. A. L. Basham, *The Wonder That Was India* (New Delhi: Picador India, 2004), 390.

2. Jadunath Sarkar, *A Short History of Aurangzib* (Hyderabad: Orient Blackswan, 2009), 36–37.

3. Subrata Dasgupta, *Awakening: The Story of the Bengal Renaissance* (New Delhi: Random House India, 2010), 31, 34.

4. Thomas Trautmann, *Arthashastra: The Science of Wealth* (New Delhi: Penguin India, 2012), 14–15.

5. Jonardon Ganeri, *Philosophy in Classical India: The Proper Work of Reason* (New Delhi: Motilal Banarasidass, 2009), 8–9.

6. Ganeri, *Philosophy in Classical India*, 8–9.

7. Ganeri, *Philosophy in Classical India*, 8–9.

8. Ganeri, *Philosophy in Classical India*, 8–9.

9. Surendranath Dasgupta, *A History of Indian Philosophy* (New Delhi: Motilal Banarasidass, 1975), 1.

10. Jonardon Ganeri, *The Lost Age of Reason: Philosophy in Early Modern India 1450–1700* (Oxford: Oxford University Press, 2011), 14, 25–26.

11. Dasgupta, *A History of Indian Philosophy*, 1.

12. Christopher Dawson, *Religion and Culture* (Washington, D.C.: The Catholic University of America Press, 2013), 74.

13. Amar Nath Prasad, *Indian Writing in English: Critical Appraisals* (New Delhi: Lotus Press, 2006), 32.

14. Mahendra Kulasrestha, ed., *Learn Rajayoga from Vivekananda* (New Delhi: Lotus Press, 2006), 32.

15. Swami Vivekananda, *The Complete Works of Swami Vivekananda*, vol. 2 (Mayavati: Advaita Ashram, 2007), 72.

16. Amiya P. Sen, *The Indispensable Vivekananda: An Anthology for Our Times* (New Delhi: Permanent Black, 2006), 220.

17. Satya P. Agarwal, *The Social Role of the Gita: How and Why* (New Delhi: Motilal Banarasidass, 1997), 70.

18. Mehdi Hasan, "Why Islam Doesn't Need a Reformation," *The Guardian* (May 17, 2015).

19. Hasan, "Why Islam Doesn't Need a Reformation."

20. Grace Morley and Arputha Rani Sengupta, *God and King: The Devaraja Cult in South Asian Art and Architecture*, The National Museum Institute Series (New Delhi: Regency, 2005), 23.

21. Ganeri, *The Lost Age of Reason*, 14, 25–26.

22. Jadunath Sarkar, *The Fall of the Mughal Empire* (New Delhi: Orient Blackswan, 2013).

23. Sarkar, *A Short History of Aurangzib*, 36–37.

24. Ganeri, *The Lost Age of Reason*, 25–26.

25. Ganeri, *The Lost Age of Reason*, 25–26.

7. ARE ALL HINDUS VEGETARIANS?

1. Makarand R. Paranjape, ed., *Swami Vivekananda: A Contemporary Reader* (New Delhi: Routledge India, 2015), 80.

2. Vivekananda, *Lectures from Colombo to Almora*, 75.

3. Mahatma Gandhi, *The Wit and Wisdom of Gandhi*, ed. Homer A. Jack (Mineola, NY: Dover Publications, 2005).

4. Vivekananda, *Lectures from Colombo to Almora*, 75.

5. Vivekananda, *Lectures from Colombo to Almora*, 82.

6. Vivekananda, *Lectures from Colombo to Almora*, 82.

7. Vivekananda, *Lectures from Colombo to Almora*, 81.

8. Ramana Maharshi, *The Teachings of Ramana Maharishi*, ed. Arthur Osborne (London: Rider Books, 2014), 38.

9. Diana L. Eck, *Banaras: City of Light* (New Delhi: Penguin India, 1992), 21.

10. http://www.greenfaith.org/religious-teachings/hindu-statements-on-the-environment.

8. HOW DO HINDUS CONSIDER THEIR OWN HISTORY?

1. Dr. Alka Pande, *Ardhanarishvara, The Androgyne: Probing the Gender Within* (New Delhi: Rupa Publications, 2004), 15.

2. Pande, *Ardhanarishvara, The Androgyne*, 15.

3. Mahatma Gandhi, *The Essence of Hinduism*, comp. and ed. V. B. Kher (Ahmedabad: Navajivan Publishing House, 2011), 12.

4. Gandhi, *The Essence of Hinduism*, 122.

5. Gandhi, *The Essence of Hinduism*, 81.

6. J. P. Vaswani, *Hinduism: What You Would Like To Know About*, comp. and ed. by Dr. Prabha Sampath and Krishna Kumari (New Delhi: New Dawn Press, 2003), 25.

7. Dorothee Enskog, "Indian Election Results Shouldn't Affect Economy Much," Credit Suisse report, April 17, 2014.

8. *OECD Economic Surveys: India 2014*, Organisation for Economic Co-operation and Development (OECD Publishing, November 2014), 73.

9. Devaki Jain and Smriti Sharma, "A Fresh Template for GDP Growth," *Gateway House* (January 1, 2015).

10. Chandra Bhan Prasad, et al., "Rethinking Inequality: Dalits in Uttar Pradesh in Market Reform Era," *Economic & Political Weekly* (August 28, 2010).

11. Shabnum Tejani, *Indian Secularism: A Social and Intellectual History, 1890–1950* (Bloomington: Indiana University Press, 2008), 81.

12. Will Durant, *Story of Civilization: Our Oriental Heritage* (New York: Fine Communications, 1997), 459.

13. Diana L. Eck, *Banaras: City of Light* (New Delhi: Penguin India, 1992), 83.

14. Eck, *Banaras: City of Light*, 83.

9. HOW DOES HINDUISM FIT INTO THE INTERNET AGE?

1. Nicholas Carr, "Is Google Making Us Stupid?" *The Atlantic* (July/August 2008).

2. Anna Lena Phillips, "The Shallows," review of *The Shallows: What the Internet Is Doing to Our Brains,* by Nicholas Carr, *American Scientist* (September/October 2010).

3. Stephen Ufford, "The Future of the Sharing Economy Depends on Trust," *Forbes* (February 10, 2015).

4. Ray Kurzweil, *The Singularity is Near* (New York: Viking, 2005), 112–113.

5. Christof Teuscher, *Alan Turing: Life and Legacy of a Great Thinker* (Berlin: Springer 2004), 406.

6. Huxley, quoted in Swami Ranganathananda, *Practical Vedanta and the Science of Values* (Belur Math: Advaita Ashrama, 2012), 102–103.

7. Hoyle, quoted in Ranganathananda, *Practical Vedanta and the Science of Values*, 74–75.

8. Swami Vivekananda, *Religion and American Cultures: An Encyclopedia of Traditions, Diversity, and Popular Expressions*, vol. 1, ed. Gary Laderman and Luis León (Santa Barbara: ABC-CLIO, 2003), 798.

9. Swami Ranganathananda, *Human Being in Depth: A Scientific Approach to Religion* (Albany: State University of New York Press, 1991), 17.

10. Swami Ranganathananda, *The Indian Vision of God as Mother* (Belur Math: Advaita Ashrama, 1992).

11. Yuval Noah Harari, "Big Data, Google and the End of Free Will," *Financial Times* (August 26, 2016).

10. A START-UP FOR THE SOUL

1. Seamus Heaney, *Opened Ground: Poems 1966–1996* (London: Faber and Faber, 2002), 11.

2. Alan Watts, "Who Wants To Be A Philosopher?" in *The Book: On the Taboo Against Knowing Who You Are* (New York: Vintage, 1989).

3. Watts, *The Book*, 152–153.

4. Watts, *The Book*, 78.

5. Peter Gay, *Modernism: The Lure of Heresy—From Baudelaire to Beckett and Beyond* (London: Vintage UK, 2009), 1.

6. Watts, *The Book*, 78.

7. Watts, *The Book*, 78.

8. Watts, *The Book*, 78.

9. Mahatma Gandhi, *The Essence of Hinduism* (Ahmedabad: Navjivan Trust, 1987), 124.

10. Gandhi, *The Essence of Hinduism*, 123–124.

11. Lewis Carroll, *Through the Looking Glass* (Adelaide: University of Adelaide, 2014).

12. Ajay Singh Almust, *Lohia: The Rebel Gandhian* (New Delhi: Mittal Publications, 1998), 5.

INDEX

ABOUT THE AUTHOR

Hindol Sengupta is an award-winning writer and journalist. He is the author of seven books. He is the youngest writer, and the only Indian, to be short-listed for the Hayek Book Prize given by the Manhattan Institute in memory of the Nobel laureate economist F. A. Hayek. He is a World Economic Forum Young Global Leader and sits on the steering committee of the Australia India Youth Dialogue. He is a Senior Fellow of the liberal think-tank Centre for Civil Society. His not-for-profit, the Whypoll Trust, has worked on gender mapping of cities and women's safety technology, and its Grin (http://www.grin.news) initiative is a storytelling platform on social enterprise which has gathered ideas from fifteen countries.